JENNY LEWIS received her PhD from the University of Melbourne in 1997. Her interest in networks and policy led to her ongoing interest in connectedness and cooperation, and to her numerous publications on policy networks, network governance and social networks. She is currently an Associate Professor in Public Policy at the University of Melbourne, where she teaches political analysis and public policy. She has also worked in state government and as a consultant. This is her third book. Her previous books are: *Health Policy and Politics: Networks, ideas and power* (IP Communications, Melbourne, 2005) and *Networks, Innovation and Public Policy: Politicians, bureaucrats and the pathways to change inside government* (co-authored with Mark Considine and Damon Alexander) (Palgrave Macmillan, Basingstoke, 2009).

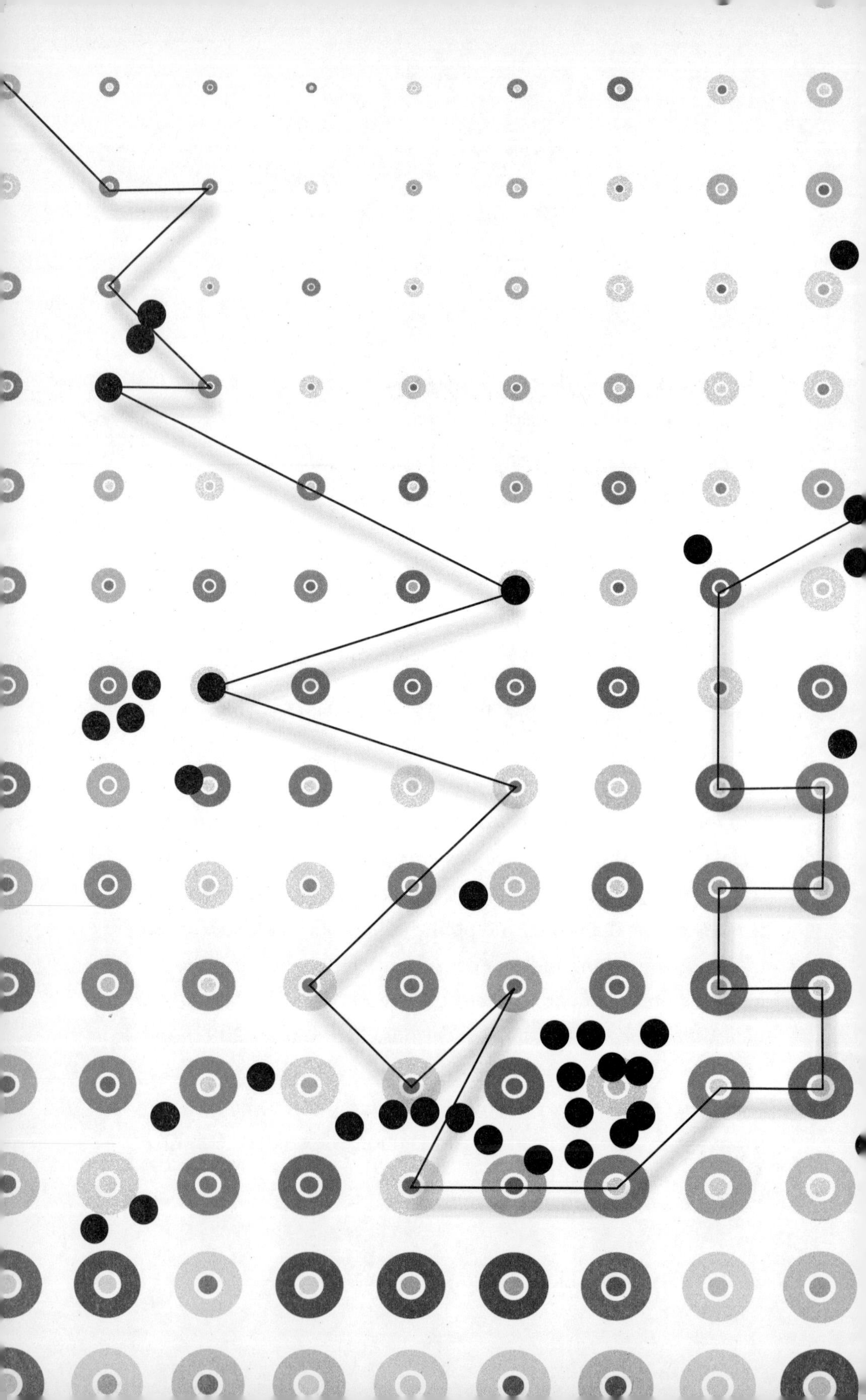

JENNY M. LEWIS

Connecting and Cooperating

SOCIAL CAPITAL and PUBLIC POLICY

UNSW PRESS

A UNSW Press book
Published by
University of New South Wales Press Ltd
University of New South Wales
Sydney NSW 2052
AUSTRALIA
www.unswpress.com.au

© Jenny M. Lewis 2010
First published 2010

10 9 8 7 6 5 4 3 2 1

This book is copyright. Apart from any fair dealing for the purpose of private study, research, criticism or review, as permitted under the Copyright Act, no part may be reproduced by any process without written permission. Inquiries should be addressed to the publisher.

National Library of Australia
Cataloguing-in-Publication entry
   Author: Lewis, Jenny M.
   Title: Connecting and cooperating: social capital and public
      policy/Jenny M Lewis.
   ISBN: 978 1 92141 013 0 (pbk.)
   Notes: Includes index.
      Bibliography.
   Subjects: Social capital (Sociology) – Government policy –
      Australia.
      Social capital (Sociology) – Australia.
      Political planning – Australia.
   Dewey Number: 361.610994

Design Di Quick
Printer Ligare
This book is printed on paper using fibre supplied from plantation or sustainably managed forests.

Published in association with the Centre for Public Policy at the University of Melbourne as the third title in the New Governance Series.

Contents

Acknowledgments 7

1 Social capital foundations 9
    Introduction 9
    Robert Putnam: The decline of social capital 14
    Pierre Bourdieu: Forms of capital and capital accumulation 25
    James Coleman: Social capital as dense social relations 30
    Nan Lin: Social capital in action 35
    Conclusions 45

2 Social capital and public policy 48
    Introduction 48
    Framework for social capital 49
    Networks and complexity 51
    The link to public policy 59
    Methodological challenges 67
    Influence, innovation, partnerships and knowledge 73

3 Influence 77
    Influence and agenda setting 80
    Network structure 85
    Influential individuals 90

    The policy agenda   94
    Issues and influential actors   99
    Dynamics and changing the agenda   100

4 Innovation   108
    Innovation within governments   110
    Network structure   113
    Centrality   118
    Key innovators   121

5 Partnerships   128
    Network governance   131
    Primary Care Partnerships   136
    Network structures   140
    Network dynamics   143
    Partnership relationships   148
    Community development partnerships   153
    Network structure   155
    The importance of brokers   159
    Conclusions   162

6 Knowledge   164
    Three levels that shape academic networks   168
    Publication networks   171
    Research networks   176
    Encouraging collaboration   182
    Proximity   185
    Conclusions   190

7 Conclusion   192
Notes   205
Bibliography   207
Index   219

Acknowledgments

In 2005, Yoshi Kashima, along with Pip Pattison and Garry Robins, convened a seminar series on social capital with their postgraduate students in Behavioural Science at the University of Melbourne, and kindly extended an invitation to me. My journey through the social capital classics began there, and it was a great introduction from a variety of different disciplinary perspectives. A few years later, when Mark Considine, the editor of this New Governance series for UNSW Press, asked if I would like to contribute to it, the choice of a topic was made easy by this previous intellectual stimulation, and the many questions about social capital that I thought remained unanswered. This book is the outcome, and my attempt to address some of the things that bothered me about how social capital was conceived in the literature, what was being claimed for it in relation to benefits, and the general silence on its link to public policy.

Writing a book on social capital alone is an ironic enterprise, and one that relies on access to embedded resources through connections to many others who are prepared to help, in numerous ways. Thom Holden provided some excellent assistance in tracking down the well-known and less well-known literature on social capital. He also deserves a special mention for his sterling work on the index of this book. Many thanks also to the rest of the small but enthusiastic network researchers in Social and Political Science at the University of Melbourne for stimulating discussions – Damon Alexander, Peta Freestone, Siobhan O'Sullivan and Sandy Ross. My thinking on social capital was vastly improved by ongoing discussions with Jeanette Pope, who has a great ability to detect academic nonsense when she hears it. Mark Considine, Yoshi Kashima and Pip Pattison all provided helpful and timely comments on draft chapters, which I am sure has improved the book immensely, but of course they are not to blame for the remaining flaws. The team at UNSW Press, from Gabriella Sterio, whose 'tough love' ensured that I actually finished the manuscript, to Sarah Shrubb, with her incredibly keen eye for less than perfect English expression, also deserve credit.

The last word of thanks must go to my partner, Stephen Ziguras. He remained engaged in innumerable conversations about the book's material and ensured that I never strayed too far from the 'so what?' questions that people actually working in the real world of policy like to ask. He also provided terrific support and understanding on the domestic front during the book-a-thon that was required for the completion of the manuscript. This book is dedicated to him, with love.

1 Social capital foundations

Introduction

'Social capital' is now part of the everyday vernacular. But linking social capital to public policy is no straightforward task. Dipping into the social capital literature to search for ways forward is fraught with definitional conflict and ideational challenges. Yet it seems that much can be gained from such an enterprise: what if we were able to bring together theories of social capital and the public policy process, to generate a framework with the dual purpose of setting out how social capital theories can be used to analyse public policy and how public policy can build social capital?

Those who know something about social capital, beyond this particular combination of two words, generally do so because of Robert Putnam's 2000 book *Bowling Alone*. The popularisation of the concept of social capital created by Putnam and others has generated – and has been generated by – a shift in public policy attention by governments in western liberal democracies, away from a firm (some would say single-minded) economic focus and towards a new framework that promises to bring the social back in. The time is ripe for a serious consideration of the term in relation to public policy. Is it really a new idea? What does it actually mean? More importantly for this book: How can it be used to understand public policy, and how can it be applied to shaping public policy interventions?

Since Robert Putnam breathed new life into social capital as an important idea, we have seen its rise and rise as a concept with crucial implications for public policy. Social capital – 'those features of social organization, such as trust, norms and networks, that can improve the efficiency of society by facilitating coordinated actions' (Putnam, Leonardi & Nanetti 1993: 167) – is now a central notion at all levels of governance, directed at a variety of outcomes. For the World Bank, the focus is on government interventions for alleviating poverty in developing countries. Economists tend to see it as enhancing efficiency, but remain concerned that government interventions to build it might 'crowd out' civil society. In the UK, the idea of the government participating in building social capital was championed by the Blair Government, because of the potential economic efficiency, equity, and civic or political benefits. In Australia, the Productivity Commission has joined the list of interested parties, and governments at all levels have searched for new ways to encourage diverse citizenries to get involved, in order to strengthen communities and generate the benefits that supposedly flow from social capital.

This interest in the concept is a good fit with the interests of the elites with whom Putnam's 'decline of social capital' thesis resonates, with a more general concern about the excesses of individualism, with a simple turning of the wheel of ideas which brings attention back to past topics, with a revalorisation of social relationships after their dismissal in the face of market ideas, and with a perceived need to reintroduce a normative dimension into a discourse which has become super-rational and hyper-technical (Schuller, Baron & Field 2000). It has appeal for contemporary policy makers because it has a hard-edged economic feel but also claims that the social is important (Halpern 2005). Each of these goes some way to explaining why Putnam's work captured the imagination of so many in government and elsewhere, and why he was able to generate and then ride a wave of interest in the topic.

Social capital has also been linked to a range of desirables – better health, less crime, higher educational achievements and even improved economic outcomes. Putnam's argument – that we need to create new structures and policies to facilitate renewed civil engagement, because 'social connectedness is one of the most powerful determinants of our well being' (2000: 326) – is an example of the type of claim that has been made by many people in many places over the last decade. Yet, despite the now large literature on social capital, and the uptake of the idea by all sectors of society and all levels of governance, the meaning of the term 'social capital' is vague, complicated and even downright dangerous, and the ways in which government might facilitate its positive aspects and valued outcomes are generally poorly articulated. It is often conflated with policy discussions about 'community'. Communities are now seen as requiring assistance or protection, because non-instrumental forms of association need defending against a dominant economic logic (Little 2002). However, this has sometimes resulted in policies aimed at 'strengthening communities' that are actually detrimental for the people concerned (Taylor 2004).

An interest in bringing clarity to the concept of social capital is not a sign that I intend to shut down discussion about what it is and is not by asserting a definition that should be applicable in all circumstances. My aim is to determine a set of principles that can be used to construct a definition that is robust and valuable for both analysing and making policy. I do not claim that such a definition will be the correct definition for every analyst or every policy problem; I actually think that there should be room for disagreement. But it is crucial to be precise about what is in scope here and what is not. This includes setting some boundaries around the notion of social capital. In analysing the concept, this book tries to take the middle path between the simplicity and parsimony of rationalism, and the complexity and nuance of constructivism (Hay 2004), and to provide a theoretically informed and empirically sensitive account of the topic.

A focus on social capital can be seen as a move to recognise the fundamental interrelatedness of everything, which is heartening to those who argue (myself included) that there is an urgent need to recognise this in public policy. We have witnessed a rise in discussions about 'wicked' problems that cross traditional portfolio boundaries, the need for joined-up solutions to policy problems, and a large and growing literature on network governance and the need for policy coordination across levels of government, across the public, for-profit and not-for-profit sectors, and across policy spheres. The central place of networks in discussions of social capital means that the concept lends itself to new ways of thinking about public policy making in a complex world. This is at the core of this book. While some have claimed that the biggest value of social capital is its heuristic value (see Schuller, Baron & Field 2000), my aim in this book is to demonstrate its value and then show how it can not only help us understand public policy but also help us shape policy solutions.

The recent public policy focus on social capital is the point from which to launch a detailed examination of its pedigree. I therefore begin with a brief overview of what Robert Putnam claimed, since he is now widely cited, as well as what some of the most severe critics of his work have counter-claimed. This starting point was chosen not as some form of entertainment, but because his claims need to be dealt with up front, as they are now almost the received wisdom on social capital – at least in the popular imagination. A substantial section of the academic literature continues to throw up criticisms of his theory, his assumptions, and his empirical approach to social capital. It is not my intention to fill vast numbers of pages with an analysis of Putnam's work. There is simply a need to outline this debate in order to move past it.

Robert Putnam: The decline of social capital

Robert Putnam's initial work on democracy in Italy provided tantalising insights that linked civic engagement to regional government performance using a series of correlations (Putnam, Leonardi & Nanetti 1993). He moved on to an examination of the US in *Bowling Alone*. In this book, he was determined to demonstrate a decline in civil society in the US, which could be proven by the decline in the number of members of voluntary associations, falling involvement in community organisations, declining sociability and social trust, and decreased engagement in voting and attending public meetings.

The definition of 'social capital' he offers is: 'connections among individuals – social networks and the norms of reciprocity and trustworthiness that arise from them' (Putnam 2000: 19). This definition suggests a strong endorsement of the importance of connections between individuals – a micro-level view of social capital. Yet his analysis is focused on group membership, which could be considered a kind of meso-level focus. And the import of what he is claiming – the decline of civil society – is focused at a higher level again, at the macro level of society. Putnam ends up talking about trust in the broadest and most general sense, which is a macro-level concept with a high level of abstraction. In the end, he has conflated all three levels (individual, organisational and societal).

Problems arise in definitions of 'social capital' that are at levels other than the individual, because of increasing abstraction and the tendency of those who focus on groups to link social capital to positive and shared outcomes. If social capital occurs only, or primarily, at the individual level, its benefits cannot logically be limited to 'public good' outcomes (Winter 2000). There is nothing to say that group actions will always be for the general good, despite this being a common assumption of social capital theories at the macro level. Defining 'social capital' as a property of groups is not necessarily wrong, but it requires a careful refinement of the concept, as Alejandro Portes (1998) observed. There are numerous benefits in defining it as a micro-level concept, as is argued throughout this chapter and the next one.

The empirical basis of Putnam's assertions has also been questioned. Pamela Paxton reviewed a range of trust and association indicators (from 1975 to 1994) that are similar to Putnam's chosen indicators (Putnam 1995a; 1995b). She concluded that trust in individuals had declined, but not trust in institutions, that membership of groups had not declined, and that time spent with neighbours and friends had changed little, although there was a shift towards more time spent with friends outside the neighbourhood (Paxton 1999).

The second part of Putnam's definition hinges on the assumption that social networks provide the (presumably positive) norms of reciprocity and trustworthiness. We are to understand from this that people expect that if they help someone, they will be helped in return, and that trust is always desirable. However, this can equally bring to mind the idea that if you do someone wrong, they will be likely to seek revenge in the future. Trust can lead to bad outcomes, as anyone who has been stung by less than scrupulous others can attest. A dramatically different view of social capital proposed by Ron Burt (2005) – 'The advantage created by a person's location in a structure of relationships' – strips away the normatively positive view of social capital that is integral to Putnam's definition. Burt's definition shares a foundation of networks/relationships with Putnam's, but little else.

James Coleman, whose work is discussed in more detail later in this chapter, also saw trust as a key component of social capital. For both Coleman and Putnam, as for many others, in order for groups of people to cooperate, they need to know each other and to expect that cooperating will be rewarded rather than exploited. Trust is seen as the lubricant which smoothes the pathways for transactions between actors (Field 2003). This provides one means of understanding how networks yield access to resources. A different view uses mutual affection as the bedrock. According to this view, to exploit the potential benefits of networks, actors have to do more than simply be in contact with each other; they need to actually enjoy each other's company (Ingram & Roberts 2000). Further, most people gain these benefits without having consciously decided to do so. They simply like being with some people and are not seeking to gain advantage through them (Kadushin 2004). Relationships are based on sentiment as well as instrumental considerations; neither of these constitutes, or necessarily creates, trust.

Clearly, there is doubt about whether trust is an integral component of social capital, or an outcome of it, or neither. Trust is itself a far from straightforward concept. Importantly, many relationships operate well on a minimal level of trust, so trust might be better seen as a separate variable, and indeed as an effect of social capital (Field 2003). I prefer to view network connections as links that may or may not generate a whole range of emotions, dispositions and outcomes, rather than focusing on trust. Trust is important, but it is not the only form of relationship that arises from network connections. Neither is it the only form of relationship of interest when examining social capital, although it is important on the expressive side of the story, along with other sentiments. It is also worth pointing out that trust may not always be desirable: mistrust can be healthy, particularly where power differentials are great.

Finally, to be linked into a social network does not automatically indicate like-mindedness or trust between actors. It means simply that there are relationships, not that these relationships are necessarily 'good' or used for the common good. They can be based on collaboration and trust, but they can equally be based on competition or obligation. Connections provide access to resources and control within a network. Burt (1992) insists that people gain advantages by exploiting informational gaps in networks. His analysis deals with a very instrumental view of social capital, centred on the benefits that accrue to individuals who know how to exploit certain positions in networks. This is a refreshing change from those who see the tie between social capital and civic benefits as a given. Links (network ties) between people merely indicate relationships; they do not necessarily indicate good relationships, and even good relationships are not good all the time.

Obviously, the same mechanisms that generate good things through social capital can also have undesirable outcomes. Portes (1998) summarised these as: excluding outsiders (the social relations that ease relations among members also restrict outsiders); making excessive claims on members (free-riding is backed by shared norms); restricting individual freedoms (through demands for conformity); and downwards levelling (individual success in areas of disadvantage disrupts group cohesion and is frowned upon). Michael Woolcock (1998) too argues that it has benefits and costs, that groups can have too little or too much of it, and that the sources of social capital required may be different as circumstances change. He sets out to resolve some of its problems by claiming that 'there are different types, levels, or dimensions of social capital, different performance outcomes associated with different combinations of these dimensions, and different sets of conditions that support or weaken favourable combinations' (Woolcock 1998: 159). Putnam, in his later work, did acknowledge that social capital can have negative consequences both for society and for members of particular networks (Schuller, Baron & Field 2000).

The concept of social capital focuses attention on the positive consequences of sociability, and calls attention to how such non-monetary forms of capital can be important sources of power and influence (Portes 1998). This reduces the distance between sociology and economics, which some find alarming, and a sign that economics is colonising the social sciences (see Fine 1999), but others see as opening up a space for dialogue across a range of disciplines (see Woolcock 1998). The World Bank has vigorously applied its own concept of social capital, which is certainly a very economics-based one: it sees social capital as something that can improve the efficiency of economic exchanges but is a second-best solution, to be used only when the law and government fail (Durlauf & Fafchamps 2004).

A systematic and fairly devastating critique of Putnam is provided by Simon Szreter (2002) in an article that demonstrates the surprising lack of examination of the historical, political, ideological and economic context in Putnam's book. Szreter points out that Putnam appears to deliberately focus on changes in a set of indicators of social capital over time without exploring how and why these changes might have occurred. His emphasis, Szreter continues, is squarely on voluntary associations, with the role of government absent from the story. This seems to suggest that civil society – and hence, in Putnam's formulation, social capital – can only be generated by an increase in membership of groups and in generalised trust at the grassroots level. In this view, governments have had no part in the alleged decline of social capital, and so have no part in rebuilding it. The potential for this to result in exhortations for the disadvantaged to pick themselves up and get connected again is worrying. As Portes (1998) notes, Putnam places the responsibility for the decline of social capital on the shoulders of individuals, rather than linking it to the economic and political changes wrought by corporations and governments.

Others have taken issue with Putnam for more normative reasons. Barbara Arneil (2006) is less than impressed with the idealised and unified American community of the past that Putnam is mourning the loss of. As she points out, Putnam's theme of a paradise lost does not resonate with the experience of historically subordinated groups such as women and cultural minorities. Indeed, she sees Putnam's call for the revival of American community as a transcendence of difference – unity, based on the values of the dominant cultural group, should be the goal. This has worrying overtones of 'sending the women back home', since it is traditionally women who take on responsibility for maintaining social relationships. It skips over the way that gender locks women into unpaid, caring and emotional networks, and the fact that these provide quite different access to resources than do men's links into public and paid networks (Warr 2006).

From a different perspective, Putnam's decline of civil society thesis can easily be seen as the unfinished business of realising justice for diverse groups who have not fared so well in the times before social capital was 'lost' (Arneil 2006). A parallel argument occurs in the literature on community. Opportunities for discussion of the common good can be seen as also creating the common good. This view is espoused by those who focus on deliberation and dialogue (Little 2002). However, a multiplicity of communities with differing values can generate disagreement and conflict (Mouffe 2000), and it may be unwise to suggest that community is a place for producing consensus.

Portes (1998), in his review of the social capital literature, distinguishes between social capital's three basic functions: as a source of social control; as a source of family support; and as a source of benefits through extra-familial networks. It is the last of these functions, he claims, that is most commonly attributed to it, and it is most often applied to examining how connections further individual mobility, such as Mark Granovetter's (1973) strength of weak ties for finding employment, Burt's (1992) structural holes created by a lack of ties, and various others who have written on dense networks as resources, following

Coleman. Portes argues for using social capital in a way that is sensitive to inequalities, and points out the need to focus on some of the distinctions made by others in exploring social capital:

> Everyday survival in poor urban countries frequently depends on close interaction with kin and friends in similar situations. The problem is that such ties seldom reach beyond the inner city, thus depriving their inhabitants of sources of information about employment opportunities elsewhere and ways to attain them (1998: 13–14).

Putnam (2000) distinguishes between bonding social capital, formed from perceived shared identity relations, and bridging social capital, formed with others from a range of backgrounds. Another way of saying this is that bonding occurs between like-minded people – or, in social network parlance, is based on homophilous ties. Bridging refers to links between different or heterogeneous people. Heterophilous ties are important in policy discussions because they are thought to be the key to social inclusion (Schuller, Baron & Field 2000). They are also more fragile and more difficult to generate because they span differences. More on the different types of social capital follows.

Some writers have claimed that attention needs to be paid to the distribution of different types of social capital. Based on an assessment of the uneven distribution of social capital of different types across socioeconomic levels (see Portes 1998; Warr 2006), the poor have more bonding and less bridging potential than the rich, and bonding social capital does not help the poor break out of poverty. The rich have much less need for bridging social capital than the poor. Szreter (2002) claims that this link to inequality is a small part of Putnam's lexicon, in which there is an emphasis on empowering the poor to bridge, rather than on inducing the rich to bridge (obviously, with others less privileged than themselves). But in his later work (Putnam & Feldstein 2003, for example), Putnam has spent time and effort mapping inequality and levels of social capital, and emphasising this distinction between bonding and bridging.

One of the more thoughtful writers on social capital as it relates to policy is Michael Woolcock. His contributions include adding linking social capital to the distinction between bonding and bridging (Woolcock 2001). Linking social capital refers to ties between unlike actors in dissimilar situations: these are ties between actors who are unalike but also unequal in power and in access to resources. They are ties in a context of vertical power relations – 'weak' in Granovetter's sense – where the differences are explicitly based on a notion of hierarchy. This reference to power brings in not just the unequal positions of different groups in society, but also the role of governments and government institutions. Social capital is not just about civil society, but also about state–civil society relations, so linking social capital helps us both think about relationships between citizens and state institutions and focus on inequality.

As Woolcock (1998) argued in a development context, in order for citizens to benefit from the use of social capital as a concept, the relations within civil society on the one hand and the institutions of the state on the other should be analysed according to the extents to which they are embedded in or autonomous from each other. Though it is easy to become bound up in definitional issues around such claims (what does 'the state' consist of? where does 'the state' end and civil society begin?), the important point here is that the role of government should be central in discussions of social capital. Szreter's criticism of Putnam includes a substantial condemnation of his lack of treatment of the role of government in building social capital. In *Bowling Alone,* Putnam has nothing to say about the role of government in building bonding social capital, and balancing it with bridging and linking social capital, which is what is required to facilitate democracy, economic efficiency and welfare functions, according to Szreter.

The concept of linking social capital concentrates attention on public policy making. To Putnam's focus on citizens and their associations in civil society it adds a need to examine the institutions of the state and other agencies that are not civil society (although as was already pointed out, that distinction can be problematic). This is hugely important for addressing the crucial questions at the heart of this book, which revolve around using social capital concepts to understand public policy and to shape it.

We can see from this inclusion of linking social capital as a third type that there is an important contrast between an approach that focuses on what civil society should do (for itself, presumably) and a bottom-up notion of how society can be reinvigorated, and one that focuses on what government should do to build social capital (top-down). This also raises some important issues about what civil society and government can do to generate social capital, and points to the need for an exploration of what type of social capital should be built in what circumstances and by whom. Clearer directions for policy analysis and interventions arise from this third type of social capital. This will be returned to in more detail later in the next chapter.

Before moving on to examine the social capital 'classics', it is worth noting that another consequence of adding this third type of social capital is that bridging and linking social capital can only grow and flourish when there is a positive endorsement of the state by its citizens. As Szreter (2002) puts it: if the message from government is 'you are on your own', why would you be motivated to engage in any kind of social capital other than bonding? Faith in institutions of the state is required for bridging and (especially) linking social capital. I leave him the final word on this:

> Social capital is not a form of do-it-yourself civic elastoplast, for patching together polities with poor systems of control and local government and depleted public services. Bonding social capital, alone, can survive in these circumstances, where it, alone, will be stimulated by even the most well-intentioned interventions. The first task in building respectful social capital in poor communities is, paradoxically, to restore collective faith in the idea of the state and in local government as a practically effective servant of the community and guarantor of personal security (Szreter 2002: 613).

Establishing a strong basis for a definition of 'social capital' requires a close examination of the social capital literature. Beyond the obvious need to review Putnam and his critics, it is no easy task to determine which of the voluminous and rapidly growing literatures should be included. My choices reflect a mixture of the scholarship that has been most often cited, the publications that have provided reviews of the literature, the authors who have had the greatest impact or offer the most insights, and the work that most explicitly links the concept directly to implications for policy making.

One review of the social capital literature begins with the following definition of 'social capital': 'social networks, the reciprocities that arise from them, and the value of these for achieving mutual goals' (Schuller, Baron & Field 2000: 1). These authors describe the seminal perspectives on the topic as coming from Pierre Bourdieu, James Coleman and Robert Putnam. The social capital classics discussed in this chapter overlap with their list and others (see Field 2003; Halpern 2005; Arneil 2006). Pierre Bourdieu and James Coleman appear in each of these as important, making them uncontroversial choices here. Some place Robert Putnam in the classic list, because of the huge influence he has had on popularising the concept. The lengthiest treatment in this book is of the less widely known Nan Lin. This is because fewer readers will be familiar with him, and because he adds a perspective that is very focused on action.

Pierre Bourdieu: Forms of capital and capital accumulation

Bourdieu generated a significant literature through his studies of multiple forms of 'capital', which began with a focus on how cultural reproduction fosters the social reproduction of class relations (Bourdieu & Passeron 1977). His work clearly links the cultural with the economic, and pays attention to the different resources available to individuals and groups of different wealth and social status. Bourdieu and his colleagues were prolific, providing theoretical claims in a number of publications. A raft of new types of capital was discussed in their writing. None of these is 'social capital', as he came to define it later. His most clearly delineated treatment defines three fundamental types of capital – economic, cultural and social (Bourdieu 1986) – and this is the focus of the following discussion.

For Bourdieu (1986), capital is accumulated labour – a force inscribed in objective or subjective structures, but also the principle underlying the regularities of the social world. It takes time to accumulate, and it creates structures of 'unequal potential' (Bourdieu 1986: 241) because it persists. Bourdieu argues that we cannot account for the structure and functioning of the social world unless forms of capital other than economic are recognised. These forms of capital are accumulated in certain ways because of historical relations of power. It is clear that the opportunities to accumulate capital are not open equally to all. Bourdieu's emphasis on social capital as an asset of the privileged, which helps them maintain their superior position, left no place for the possibility that the less privileged might also gain benefits from social ties (Field 2003).

Bourdieu (1986) argued that we need to grasp capital and profit in all their forms, as it is not only the exchange of goods that is important. He also saw it as crucial to establish laws whereby different types of capital (power) change into one another. He described capital as having three guises: economic (money, property), cultural (educational qualifications) and social (obligations and connections, titles of nobility) (Bourdieu 1986). Economic capital is immediately convertible, while cultural and social capital are less immediately convertible, and only convertible in certain cases.

For Bourdieu, cultural capital means the personal gains brought by education (akin to human capital in most definitions), but also the contribution education makes to the reproduction of social structure. It is accumulated by an individual agent, and declines and dies with its bearer. It is external wealth converted into an integral part of a person that cannot be transmitted by gift or purchase. But it also acquires value through its position in the distribution of capital. That is, there is advantage to be gained from being able to read when others are illiterate, or, in a higher level example, having a postgraduate degree when the majority have undergraduate degrees. The link between economic and cultural capital is the time needed to acquire the latter, which those with more economic capital have more ability to accumulate.

Bourdieu defines social capital as follows:

> Social capital is the aggregate of the actual or potential resources which are linked to possession of a durable network of more or less institutionalised relationships of mutual acquaintance and recognition – or in other words, to membership in a group – which provides each of its members with the backing of the collectively-owned capital, a 'credential' which entitles them to credit, in the various senses of the word (1986: 248–49).

The network basis for Bourdieu's definition of social capital is clear in this definition, and in his writing on the different forms of capital and how they are mobilised. He argues that the amount of social capital held by an actor depends on the size of the network of connections s/he can mobilise, and on the volume of capital of different forms possessed by each of those to whom s/he is connected. This clarion statement of the importance of both network size and the differential resources that might be generated through different ties is worth committing to memory. A network of connections is necessary to produce and reproduce lasting, useful relationships that generate material and other profits.

Bourdieu is also keenly focused on the idea that social capital accumulation, like the accumulation of other forms of capital, is an unequal process. Many institutions are designed to favour legitimate (which most often means homogeneous) exchanges and to exclude others. It is also clear that in Bourdieu's theory, in addition to the forms of capital being linked, economic capital is at the root of all other types of capital. It can be turned into other forms of capital, but only with costs. While some goods and services can be obtained immediately with economic capital, others can only be obtained by virtue of social capital, and even then not instantaneously unless the relationships have been long established and maintained, as if for their own sake. Bourdieu (1986) argues that social capital produces its best effects in direct proportion to the extent to which the fact that economic capital is at its root remains hidden.

Clearly, the processes that bring about social capital are less transparent and more uncertain than those that produce economic capital, and are characterised by unspecified obligations, uncertain time horizons and a possible lack of reciprocity (Portes 1998). It is these characteristics of social capital that have tipped many authors over into the normatively positive view of social capital that ties it to trust. But it is not necessary to make this leap of faith. The strength of Bourdieu's theory is that it is based on examining networks and resources. It does not require the transformation of connectedness into trust and shared norms, à la Putnam. This conflation of networks and trust needs to be put to rest, as does the notion that social capital is inherently good. We only need to think more carefully about power and inequality as factors that underlie and shape trust relations, just as they underlie network relations, to see that a much better starting point for thinking about social capital is to avoid the assumption that networks generate trust always and for everyone.

Neither is it necessary to take the extreme rational choice position that investment in social capital is best conceived of as a calculated pursuit of gain, when it is more likely to be experienced as an emotional investment (both necessary and disinterested). Bourdieu (1986) argues that it is erroneous to see the choices that lead a person to act in a certain way as a rational strategy based on cynical calculation. More recently, others have pointed out that the value of social capital as a concept is that it brings to attention aspects of social relations that are not easily or convincingly incorporated into models based on rationalism and self-interest (Edwards & Foley 1998).

Bourdieu's analysis is one of the most theoretically refined. Portes (1998) and others credit the lack of attention paid to his work as related to his writing in French and the time that passed before English translations appeared. But perhaps it is not surprising that Coleman and Putnam virtually ignored him, given his different conceptualisation. Bourdieu's treatment of social capital comes from an instrumental point of view, focused on the benefits that accrue to individuals through their connections, and on the deliberate construction of certain patterns of relations. His definition clearly distinguishes between the social relationship itself, which provides actors with claims to the resources of others, and the amount and quality of those resources (Portes 1998). His work also makes it clear that social capital is not a benign force, working equally in the interests of all. It draws boundaries around and between people, often reconstructing existing power differentials (Arneil 2006). This is a long way from Putnam's aggregated norms, and trust-based and public good version of social capital.

James Coleman: Social capital as dense social relations

James Coleman's studies of social capital are said to have come from an interest in drawing together the disciplines of sociology and economics. He argued that social capital was as important as human capital, and defined social capital as 'the set of resources that inhere in family relations and in community social organization and that are useful for the cognitive and social development of a child or a young person' (Coleman 1994: 300).

This definition reflects the American sociologist's interest in education, but it can be easily generalised. The salient points are first, that social capital is something that inheres in the structure of relations between actors, and second, that it provides access to valued resources. He viewed social capital as functional, constituting useful resources for actors through connections which establish obligations, expectations and trust, create information channels, and set norms backed by sanctions (Coleman 1988). It is productive, like other forms of capital, making the achievement of certain ends possible.

Coleman's definition feeds directly into more recent definitions of social capital that claim it is composed of a network, a group of norms and values, and a set of sanctions that help maintain the norms and network (Halpern 2005). I find this three-component version of social capital unhelpful and unconvincing. Sanctions seem to be the flipside of norms, which are inherently positive in this definition, as they relate only to those cases where social capital rests on a 'public good' assumption – at least in Halpern's formulation.

Along with Bourdieu, Coleman provides an exemplar of social capital theory that is at the individual level, but also has collective aspects. But for Coleman, social capital is a largely unproblematic concept – a functional means through which ends are achieved (Arneil 2006). In contrast to Bourdieu, Coleman sees social capital creation as a largely unintentional process, arising from activities intended for other purposes (Schuller, Baron & Field 2000). His particular interest in families and educational attainment means that he focused on closure and dense networks. This is a quite different emphasis from more recent focuses in the social capital literature, in which joining and openness are the central concerns.

Burt (2005) claims that authors as diverse as Bourdieu, Coleman and Putnam have all agreed that social capital is a metaphor for social structure, and defines a form of capital that generates advantages for some individuals and groups. Burt is certainly interested in closure, to the extent that it reinforces the status quo, since those at odds with the preferences in a closed network will be chastised. Closure in networks protects relations within them and amplifies strong relations (Burt 2005). However, he also emphasises the brokerage aspect of networks that reaches outside this closure, and points to the competitive advantage to be gained if you are the link between otherwise unconnected actors or groups – his concept of structural holes – that allows access to different resources.

Different motivations can be seen as underpinning these two different versions of social capital, with Coleman emphasising closure and density in networks to provide support and resources, and Burt emphasising bridging and loose networks as providing opportunities for entrepreneurs. Kadushin (2004) points out that brokers need support and a way of reaching out to make connections, and claims that these two motives and both network forms co-exist. Nan Lin's distinction between homophilous and heterophilous ties, used respectively for expressive and instrumental purposes, corresponds to this and is further explored in the next section.

Coleman's contribution, like Bourdieu's, has been very influential. These two authors both highlighted the importance of the concept of social capital in examining how elites use their contacts to reproduce their status – albeit from very different starting points. Coleman highlighted the importance of social capital in providing access to resources, as did Bourdieu. However, Coleman's work does not have the explicit class structural analysis of Bourdieu, so it obscures the distinction between resources themselves and the ability to obtain them through membership of groups (Portes 1998).

Theories of social capital that refer to the accumulation and use of resources help strip away the normatively positive gloss that coats many contemporary discussions of social capital. If social capital is about people using resources to achieve desired ends, then clearly it is not always 'good'. Being well connected in a racist, violent or criminal group might increase your feeling of belonging, the number of friends you have, and so on, but it does not produce anything good for those outside your group, and is likely to have damaging consequences for some inside as well. Using the term 'resources' helps with this, because it has neither negative nor positive connotations, but simply refers to a means that can be used to achieve an end – either good or bad. Of course it also follows that the outcomes might be positive for some and negative for others.

As Deb Warr (2006) records, most social capital theories lack either a gender or a class analysis. Bourdieu developed social capital within an analysis of class processes, but he did not try to account for how disadvantaged people might derive benefits from their social relations. The need for the poor to access social support through their networks to 'get by' (bonding), rather than accessing social capital to 'get ahead' (bridging), points to a conclusion that levels of socioeconomic advantage are related to the types of networks that are important. Socioeconomic status is linked to locality, and the resultant spatial patterns yield clusters of people who are similarly advantaged or disadvantaged (see Massey 1996). This helps lock people into networks with those of the same class, and makes bonding by far the most likely form of connection. People who are unemployed tend to end up in networks of other unemployed people (Onyx & Bullen 2001; Field 2003), and it is hard for them to break out of this in the absence of weak ties (Granovetter 1973), or ties to those with high occupational status (Volker & Flap 1999). As others have demonstrated empirically (see Russell 1999; Warr 2005; Warr 2006), for the disadvantaged, the distinction between bonding and bridging networks is acute, whereas these networks are likely to overlap significantly for those who are more advantaged, and who also have a greater ability to form helpful connections.

It was not Coleman's purpose to pay attention to the distribution of social capital. But it is clear that we should, in the same way that we pay attention to the distribution of economic and human capital. It is worth noting that this distribution can be uneven between individuals within a group, as well as between groups. In the end, it is only possible to say if social capital is positive or negative in relation to outcomes, and then the issue of outcomes for whom also needs to be resolved. Portes (2000) has spent some effort on this, arguing that at an individual level, social capital is clearly linked to a person's networks and the (separate) material and informational benefits that accrue to them through these. At the collective level, where much social capital work is focused, this separation of networks from benefits is lacking, contributing to the circularity of arguments that social capital produces better government and policy, and that better government and policy produces social capital. Coleman sees collective social capital as aiding individuals, as does Bourdieu. Nan Lin concentrates on individuals, as we shall see.

Nan Lin: Social capital in action

In order to be able to make a link from social capital to public policy, we need theories of social capital that include action. While it is possible to look just at potential resources when we think about policy, it is important to be able to show how these resources matter, and how they can be used to improve society.

Nan Lin's 2001 book *Social Capital: A theory of social structure and action*, as the title suggests, examines action as a central part of the equation. For Lin, social capital is more than a potential resource, more than a stockpile of something that people accumulate and do not spend. It is a resource that is used purposively to achieve a desired end. People use their networks as a means of support or advice, for gathering information, and to pursue valued outcomes. The accumulation of connections to others without the use of them amounts to unrealised potential for Lin. His theory of social capital is, to a much larger extent than the other theories described here (with the exception of Burt), one of rational choice, and one that is not just about potential, but about the actual use of resources to achieve something.

Lin claims that social capital is best understood by examining the mechanisms and processes by which embedded resources in social networks are captured as investment. These mechanisms and processes help bridge the gap in understanding the macro-micro linkage between structure and individuals. A considerable amount of time is spent outlining theories of capital in the first chapter of the book. He refers to Marx's theory as the classic theory of capital, since the basic idea that capital is the investment of resources for the production of profit has remained in all subsequent theories of capital. He summarises Marx's important ideas as follows (Lin 2001: 7). First, capital is intimately associated with the production and exchange of commodities. Second, capital involves processes as well as commodities. Third, any capital that results from these processes is an added value (surplus or profit). Fourth, capital is intrinsically a social notion, entailing social activity, Fifth, capital is by definition in the hands of those who control the means of production, and so can only be accumulated by them.

He then goes on to describe two versions of neo-capital theory: human capital and cultural capital. Human capital assumes that capital can rest with the individual worker. Human capital is the value added to workers when they acquire knowledge, skills, and other assets useful to the employer in the processes of production and exchange. It is the added value embedded in the workers themselves, making it distinct from physical capital (Lin 2001: 8–9).

While the concept of human capital is consistent with a Marxist analysis, since capital is still viewed from the perspective of the producer, it is also a major challenge to it, as when workers acquire skills and other capital to increase their value, they have mobility. Social structure is no longer a rigid two-class system but a hierarchy of grades of capitalists, with mobility between classes possible (Lin 2001: 10). Human capital theory deviates substantially from classical Marxist theory, as it focuses on workers and sees them as potential investors. It follows that there is a blurring of the division between classes, as workers can become capitalists.

In describing cultural capital, Lin contrasts it with human capital's emphasis on the free will or self-interest of workers. Cultural capital is based on symbolism and meaning, and so concentrates on social practice and social reproduction. Bourdieu's work on symbolic violence by the dominant class argues that the culture and values of the dominant class are legitimated as the culture and values of society. They are 'misrecognised' as the culture and values of the entire society, and are not seen as things that sustain the dominant class and subordinate others (Bourdieu & Passeron 1977). This is consistent with Marx, as it reflects the imposition of one class's values on another. But Bourdieu adds insights about the internalisation of the dominant values and culture (habitus). Thus the dominant group remains a pervasive force in all classes in Bourdieu's analysis. Lin argues that Bourdieu sees society as 'a network of positions, the better ones of which are struggled over' (2001: 16).

Lin summarises the change from classical to neo-capital theories as a shift from the macro (societal) to the micro (individual) level, without ruling out the effects of the macro level, as including action or choice as important, and as stressing the interplay of individual actions and structural positions in the capitalisation process. All of these are important shifts, and all contribute to Lin's own theory of social capital.

Social capital as capital captured through social relations is the focus of the second chapter of Lin's book. He begins it with the statement that the premise behind the notion of social capital is 'investment in social relations with expected returns in the marketplace' (Lin 2001: 19), citing a number of authors whose definitions are consistent with this. Both human capital and cultural capital see capital as resources invested and vested in individual actors. Social capital is an advance, Lin maintains, because it is the capital captured through social relations – that is, through connections and access to resources in networks. Some people do better than others. The human capital explanation for this is that the people who do better are more able. The social capital explanation is that some do better because they are better connected. Social capital and human capital are both thus set to work to explain advantage (Burt 2005).

Lin goes on to discuss why embedded resources in social networks enhance the outcomes of actions. First, the flow of information is facilitated, because social ties provide useful information in imperfect markets, reducing transaction costs. Second, these social ties may exert influence on those who play critical decision-making roles involving an individual. Third, social ties may be seen as certifications of an individual's social credentials, reflecting his/her access to resources through social networks. Fourth, social relations reinforce identity and recognition. Lin claims that these four elements – information, influence, social credentials and recognition – may explain why social capital works in instrumental (outcome-driven) and expressive (recognition and acknowledgment) ways that are not accounted for by physical or human capital (2001: 20).

As has already been reported and will be returned to later, there are differences between social capital theories according to the level at which returns are conceived. Some see social capital as accumulating to individuals – either as gaining returns in instrumental actions, or preserving gains in expressive actions. In these theories, the basic unit of analysis is the individual and how they invest in social relations and capture the embedded resources in them to generate returns (Lin 2001: 21). A distinction can also be made between personal resources, which individuals hold, and social resources, which are those accessed through an individual's social connections (Lin 1982). Some individual-level versions focus on the resources generated by connections to others who have strong relations with an individual.

Bourdieu, Coleman and Putnam all see social capital as accumulating at the group level, according to Lin. They all examine how certain groups develop and maintain social capital as a collective asset and how this enhances their life chances. Bourdieu sees social capital as a form of capital produced by group members, which allows them credit. Coleman sees it as the resources, real or potential, gained from relationships. Lin argues that for both of these theorists, dense or closed networks are the means by which collective capital can be maintained and reproduced. Putnam follows this focus, argues Lin. However, he does recognise, as have others, the significant point of departure between Putnam and Coleman, who see social capital as a public good, and Bourdieu, who sees it as a class or privilege good.

Seeing social capital as something that accumulates to groups should not be confused with the level at which social capital is theorised. As noted earlier, both Bourdieu and Coleman have provided individual-level theories of social capital that include collective aspects, and this is their strength. Lin argues that there is an emerging consensus from Portes, Burt and himself that social capital, as a theory-generating concept, should be conceived in the social network context. Both Bourdieu and Coleman have also done this, and this is one of the reasons why they are included in this book. For Lin, social capital is 'the resources embedded in social networks accessed and used by actors for actions' (2001: 25). The important principles encapsulated in this definition are that social capital represents resources embedded in social relations rather than in individuals, that the access and use of resources resides with individual actors, and that action rather than potential is central.

Many agree that social capital benefits both collectives and individuals. Problems arise when this is conflated with discussions of collective or public goods. Lin makes the point that although social capital is a relational asset, it should be distinguished from collective assets such as culture, norms and trust: 'Divorced from its roots in individual interactions and networking, social capital becomes merely another trendy term to employ or deploy in the broad context of improving or building social integration and solidarity' (2001: 26). This is indeed what has occurred over the last decade. He also believes that the requirement for network density or closure found in Bourdieu, Coleman and Putnam is not necessary or realistic. A better focus, he claims, is bridges in networks, following Granovetter

(1973) and Burt (1992). Lin notes that for preserving or maintaining resources, denser networks may have an advantage, but for searching for and obtaining resources, bridges should be more useful. This has an obvious resonance with the bonding and bridging distinction discussed earlier in this chapter.

In his third chapter, which deals with the structural foundation for his theory of social capital, Lin describes how meanings and significance are assigned to resources, based on three assumptions. These are that they are assigned by consensus or influence which signals their relative values, that all actors take actions to promote their self-interest by maintaining and gaining valued resources when opportunities arise, and that maintaining and gaining valued resources are the two primary motives for action, with the former outweighing the latter. Lin's is clearly a theory of social capital based on rational choice – value-maximising individuals making rational decisions about what will benefit them. He acknowledges that actors have different resources, and accepts that those with more are more likely to be involved in decisions about those resources, and that their self-interest is usually served particularly well because it is consistent with the collective interest, which is shaped by their own values (Lin 2001: 31). He also claims that powerful individuals can further advance their standing by either gaining more resources or manipulating value consensus to promote the value of resources they have or can access.

In Lin's definition of social structure, positions have different amounts of valued resources, and are hierarchically related based on authority (the control of and access to resources). They share rules and procedures in the use of resources, which are entrusted to agents who act on these rules and procedures. This highlights the fact that some resources are embedded in positions, and others are possessed by individuals. Authority relates to control over and access to valued resources, and rules guide behaviour and interactions, which leads to structural stability. The selection of occupants favours those who 'fit' the structure, but individuals still have opportunities to act (Lin 2001: 34). In other words, they have agency.

Social networks represent a less formal structure than hierarchy. A network is fluid, and it may evolve naturally or be socially constructed for a particular purpose. Lin claims that network interactions should be analysed and understood as both relationship patterns among actors and as resource patterns. Interaction occurs primarily when there is shared emotion. The homophily (like-me) hypothesis is an extension of this: social interactions tend to take place among individuals with similar lifestyles and socioeconomic characteristics. Lin concludes that interactions tend to link together actors with similar social positions and similar resources. That is, similar actors will be closer in social structures and will also have access to similar embedded resources.

In his chapter on the action foundation of social capital, Lin notes that it is rooted in social networks and social relations. Conceived of as resources embedded in a social structure that are accessed purposively, it consists of structure (embeddedness), opportunity (accessibility through social networks) and action (use) (Lin 2001: 41).

This focus on action sets Lin apart from other social capital theorists, and it is here that he makes extensive use of social network theory. He discusses personal resources as human capital – those things in the possession of individuals. Personal resources are fully owned by an individual actor (education, for example), but others, such as those attached to a certain position, are not. Ownership expires when the individual actor moves out of that position. The importance of network ties is that an individual can gain access to the resources held by others through them. These ties have important symbolic value, even if they are not mobilised, and can enhance an actor's social standing simply because they are known about. In summary, resources can be accessed through direct and indirect ties, and they may be either personal or positional. Hence, an actor's social capital extends as far as his/her social networks.

Lin assumes that valued resources are maintained in order to promote expressive action – acknowledgment and sharing with no action beyond this asked for or expected. The motive to seek and gain additional resources triggers instrumental action involving others in order to achieve a goal. Expressive action which seeks to maintain existing resources is expected to take precedent over instrumental action, since losing existing resources is a greater threat than not gaining additional resources, according to Lin's theory.

Having distinguished between personal and positional resources and expressive and instrumental action, Lin makes a further distinction in relation to similarity. The homophily principle leads to an expectation that social interactions will occur most frequently among individuals of similar status. Relating this to action, Lin argues that both partners in a heterophilous interaction have to make a greater effort in forging the interaction than those in a homophilous interaction, and that these are therefore less likely to occur. Heterophilous interactions require more effort because of resource differentials and lack of shared sentiment. Homophilous interactions promote sentiment and shared resources. This resonates both with the strong and weak ties argument and with the bonding and bridging distinction.

Lin makes even more explicit the effect of this principle in relation to action and gaining resources, and his rational choice credentials shine through strongly here. Heterophily is required to gain new resources, he postulates; this resonates with Burt's (1992) claims about the competitive advantage of occupying structural holes, and Granovetter's (1973) theory of the additional resources that can be accessed through weak ties. That is, obtaining additional or better resources requires interacting with actors in other and better positions so that better information or authority can be obtained. Further, the best payoff comes from interacting with others who have access to different resources, and/or more resources themselves. Naturally, if you are already highly placed, you stand to gain little by seeking out different others. For the well off, heterophilous interactions may offer low returns, since energy is spent on connecting to others without the payoff of greater access to resources.

Is social capital purposive action or simply the structural opportunity present for an actor? Lin claims that Bourdieu sees structural constraints on opportunities as decisive. Coleman sees social capital as the function it serves for a particular purpose and a particular actor. If something embedded in the structure works for an individual for a particular action then it is social capital. Granovetter (1973) points to the process of gaining information through weak ties, but Lin does not specifically argue that actors are conscious of having an advantage because of the network positions they occupy, and hence the access to resources they have. Burt (1992) is silent on action, despite his focus on opportunities provided by network structures, and an assumption that they will be used to achieve desired outcomes. Lin claims to make explicit the hints of purposive action made by Granovetter and Burt in his own theory of social capital, emphasising that social structure and action are mutually reinforcing. While structures constrain actors, actors also can and do change structures using the resources they have at their disposal, and it is this that Lin emphasises more than other writers in this field.

Conclusions

In this chapter I have surveyed the work of some major theorists of social capital. Nan Lin's work has featured here because it provides a firm footing and because it is less well known than other social capital theories. However, it takes us only so far, particularly in our thinking about governments and public policy processes. I can now map out the contours for a framework of social capital to take into the second chapter. The first part of that framework is that it is best seen as an individual-level concept, and should incorporate networks as a distinguishing and crucial feature. In addition, a good theory of social capital will operate at more than one level and permit consequences at more than one level, allowing for the benefits to flow to groups and even whole societies, as long as the focus of analysis is individual.

A concept of social capital should not include the normatively positive aspect that some theories of it have included, and should not assume that the outcomes for groups will always be desirable. Rational choice is a strong theoretical footing to begin from, and this is the strength of Lin's book. But social capital theory also needs to incorporate social and political perspectives, rather than relying purely on economic assumptions. Sentiments are involved in interactions between people. This adds an important dimension to a value-maximising, opportunity and advantage-seeking definition, and points to the need to explore the more expressive purposes that networks serve in addition to those that are more instrumental. Another important set of distinctions relates to network-based concepts that highlight the importance of bonding/bridging/linking, strong/weak and homophilous/heterophilous ties. Levels and forms are interrelated, so an individual analysis cannot tell the whole story; neither will a focus on only one form of social capital.

Social capital being a multi-level concept, which can be conceived of at the micro (individual), meso (group or organisation) or macro (societal) level, means that we can understand it as having meaning at the level of individuals, groups and societies. We can also see its benefits as accumulating at any of these levels. In addition, these levels are interrelated, so social capital at one level can affect and be affected by social capital at other levels.

Social capital theory should be explicit about action, as well as about structure. Focusing on embedded resources is a good start, but a concept that is of use for understanding policy and directing policy proposals needs to incorporate agency, in order to think about what can be achieved and how it can be achieved. It should have a strong time dimension to it, since what distinguishes social capital from other forms of capital is the length of time it takes to accumulate. It should not confuse cause with effect, or lapse into tautological statements, but should keep a firm grip on the differences between potential resources and outcomes that are achieved. However, it also needs to recognise that cause and effect cannot be entirely disentangled, as they are interdependent.

The next chapter is concerned with incorporating network and complexity theories into the concept. The methodological challenges associated with framing social capital in this way are explored and a case is made for the importance of using relational data. The link to analysing policy and directing policy interventions is explicated, and the four illustrative cases included in this book are outlined.

2 Social capital and public policy

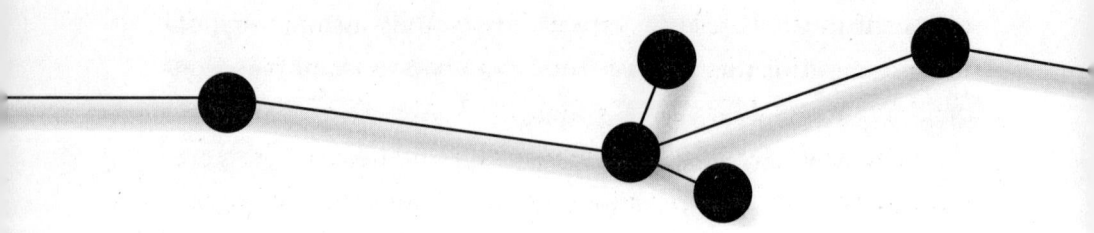

Introduction

The term 'social capital' has been so liberally applied to so many different aspects of life that it now means both everything and nothing. Some firm boundaries are required to contain this sprawl, and capture what is essential to it and unique about it. Nan Lin's (2001) definition of social capital – as the resources embedded in social networks accessed and used by actors for actions – is a strong basis. But it is important to recognise that simply being connected is a resource in itself. Social capital should be seen as arising from both the connections themselves and the purposes to which they are put (both the means and the ends). To focus on the payoffs that accrue from relationships (instrumental outcomes) to the exclusion of the more expressive elements of them is a mistake. The major modification

I suggest to a rational choice version of social capital is to dial down the purposefulness and recognise that connections are more than just potential links to resources, but are resources in and of themselves.

There is something strange but compelling about Paldam's (2000) definition of social capital as the glue generating excess cooperation (that is, cooperation that exceeds assumptions of individual rationality). It takes an economist to frame it in this way. Again, his definition highlights the strength of anchoring the concept in rational action, while simultaneously drawing our attention to the shortcomings of definitions that do not reflect the innate sociability of most humans.

Let me now move to thinking about what is important to investigate about the concept. A good starting list is the extent to which these resources incur advantages, and to whom, and under what circumstances, and what network shapes these resources assume when they are accessed (Kadushin 2004). The set of principles that I think should be embodied within the concept are presented below, grouped into a number of aspects.

Framework for social capital

Levels:

- It is best conceived of at the individual level.
- It is about individuals in networks.
- Its benefits can accrue to individuals and collectives.
- It is a multi-level concept (micro, meso, macro).
- There are interactions between levels.

Forms and types of ties:
- There are different forms of it (bonding, bridging, linking).
- It is based on both instrumental and expressive/sentiment ties.
- Ties have meaning in and of themselves.
- There are interactions between forms.

Accumulation and use:
- It takes time to accumulate.
- It is about action as well as structure.
- Causes and consequences are separate but interlinked.
- There are interactions between levels and forms.
- Its consequences are neither inherently positive nor inherently negative.

The parameters listed here make clear the need for social capital to have a strong foundation in network theory, because of the focus on relations, and in complexity theory, because of the interactions. With this set of parameters established, the remainder of this chapter uses them to guide a discussion of networks, complexity, and the link to public policy, by drawing boundaries around the field of social capital and focusing only on the most pertinent literature. Having laid down the framework for the levels at which social capital should be conceived, the forms and types of ties that are involved, and how social capital is accumulated and used, these principles are then built into a discussion of methodological challenges. The chapter concludes with an overview of the four empirical cases that follow, which aim to illustrate how social capital affects public policy and how public policy can affect social capital.

Networks and complexity

Like 'social capital', the term 'networks' has spread inexorably. The network literature encompasses network governance, policy networks, issue networks, and networks as a form of management, through to actor network theory, social network analysis, and the network society. A first important distinction can be made between the network as a conceptual model, and as a form of coordination and governance (Thompson 2003). A further distinction within networks as a conceptual model is the key difference between the network as theory and the network as an analytical technique (Lewis 2005a). The first provides a means for thinking about interconnectedness and the second provides tools for analysing it. Both the network as a concept and the network as a tool are important here, the first for strengthening the concept of social connectedness and the second for coming to grips with the all-important task (for public policy) of measuring it.

Networks, as a mode of governing deliberately (Kickert, Kiljn & Koppenjan 1997) or as a metaphor for the reality of contemporary governing (Rhodes 1997; Kooiman 2003), are crucial in relation to specific policies that aim to join things up through, for example, partnerships (examined in Chapter 5) and collaborations (Chapter 6). Networks that are more self-organising and informal, in the sense that they have not been imposed or encouraged through policy signals and governance arrangements, are also of interest. The emphasis in Chapters 3 and 4 is on how these networks impact on the policy process. This kind of analysis of the public policy process adds another layer to the more formal institutional and interest-based analyses of standard political science. Of course, this distinction between top-down governance networks and bottom-up self-generated networks is an artificial one between two polar extremes; all networks are somewhere on a continuum from more to less structured, and the structures of all are shaped by contextual factors. This applies as much to the most open, informal networks as to designed networks, none of which can completely overcome the relationships and established understandings already in existence.

Networks of all types consist of a set of nodes (individual or organisational actors) linked by some form of individual or interorganisational relationship (or tie), and delineated by some specific criteria. The important question then is what represents a node, a tie or a boundary (Diani 2003) in different formulations. A number of different approaches have been used to research networks. Systems accounts emphasise sets of connections between actors that establish typical relationship patterns, which in turn shape an organisation's ability to achieve things (Emery & Trist 1965). In these accounts, organisations are embedded in sets of relationships that tend to lock actors into customary forms of interaction (Marsden 1981). Policy networks operate at a similar (meso) level. Social networks focus on individuals.

Policy networks are configurations of individuals and organisations engaged in a policy sector (Rhodes & Marsh 1992). They have been conceptualised as coalitions, corporatist institutions or professional monopolies, and are defined in terms of resource sharing. To enter these policy networks, individuals need to invest in learning the group language, establishing relationships, and even subscribing to a certain policy paradigm (Lewis 1999). This does not imply that connections are based on trust or cooperation; it indicates only that to be part of the network, some meanings must be shared.

These interest group or resource dependence networks rest on functional interdependence, where no single actor determines any outcome unilaterally – what matters is the 'actor constellation' (Scharpf 1997). The literature on policy networks concentrates on understanding how groups, linked into semi-formal and ongoing relationships, control the policy process (Benson 1982). Nodes are generally seen as organisations, and ties are based on shared activities and resources (which can be based on conflict rather than cooperation), and the boundary is set by the analyst. This stops short of revealing the arrays of formal and informal connections among individuals.

In summary, the 'network' is commonly being used as a central metaphor in policy and governance literature, from research which views individual actors as influencing policy through their interests and resources, embedded within communication and resource-exchange networks (Laumann & Knoke 1987) to 'network governance' driven by a dynamic which is multi-agency, complex and increasingly difficult to steer (Rhodes 1997). This literature sometimes spills over into consideration of increasing organisational and community input to considerations of public policy aimed at building social capital, but rarely does it explicitly engage with social capital theory.

Social network approaches are close to social capital theories that are conceived of at the individual level, because they focus on interpersonal ties among individuals. Nodes are individual people and ties are direct personal interactions or connections, based on some criteria of interest. These relations (ties) can be single or multiple and may also differ in terms of direction, content, intensity (frequency) and strength. In policy networks, these ties do not automatically indicate like-mindedness or trust. Boundaries can be defined by the analyst's view of which groups are involved, or through an empirical assessment of those people who are actually connected to each other somehow (Diani 2003).

Some important social network concepts and organising principles have already been described in Chapter 1. Lin (2001) and others before him (see McPherson & Smith-Lovin 1987) have argued that network ties are more likely to be found where there is homophily. Homophilous ties are more common, and are used to maintain existing resources. Relationships with others like ourselves are also the easiest to form. In Bourdieu's analysis, homophily helps maintain the status quo of those who are similarly placed in society because of their resources. Gaining access to extra resources requires heterophilous ties; most people have fewer of these. They take more energy to establish, but can provide the biggest gains because they reach beyond the ties that provide access to 'more of the same'.

One of the most important papers in this field is Mark Granovetter's (1973) seminal work on strong and weak ties, and his conclusion that unemployed people need to be able to move beyond their own milieu in order to find employment. Heterophily is desirable for those with fewer resources, who have incentives to bridge vertically upwards to those with more resources. But what incentives are there to bridge downwards? Woolcock's linking social capital concept demonstrates the application of this to public policy, with government being able to help the poorest in society through implementing policies that bridge downwards to build social capital.

In addition to Lin and Granovetter, Burt's work is very strongly network-based. He coined the phrase 'structural holes' to designate a particular network position. In his rational choice and competition-based view of social capital, actors have social capital by dint of their network positions, when they bridge structural holes by accessing actors that others cannot. As Burt (1992) argues, someone in the position of 'the third who benefits' can decide to whom, when, and in what form information will be disclosed. Clearly this is a position of power, created by a network structure. Such actors exercise control in networks, because their positions bridge the gaps in disconnected social structures. Occupying a structural hole can yield resources in the service of either the self (as Burt suggests) or others in the network, or in the service of the network as a whole. In his later work, Burt (2005) focused on brokerage and closure, and argued that far more compelling results could be obtained from social capital studies if attention shifted away from metaphors, and focused instead on concrete network mechanisms.

A discussion of networks leads naturally into a discussion of complexity. Social capital is relational, and it follows that cause and effect become blurred as we look at things from different angles simultaneously in order to capture the changing nature of relationships. Actors and actions should be seen as interdependent, rather than dependent, and as interacting and reinforcing rather than being linked in a unidirectional sequence from causes to consequences. Those last words lead directly to complexity theory, which holds some promise for dealing with the circularity that Portes (1998; 2000) wants us to be rid of. Complexity theory provides a new way of thinking about interconnected systems. The question is, does this scientific theory have any relevance to debates about social capital? And perhaps even more importantly, can it help in thinking about how public policy is made and in setting directions for how it should be made?

Interaction and complexity are now central concepts that define the world we live in. The fundamental importance of social networks to social capital poses challenges to the dominance of simple and sequential models of understanding and analysing social capital. The circularity in much that is written about social capital in its collective forms makes it difficult to say whether it should be seen as a characteristic of a flourishing society or a means of achieving it. Yet the world is complex – both in the popular usage of the term, which means 'things are complicated', and in its scientific usage, which indicates that we live in a non-linear world of multiple and contingent causation which is about non-order (rather than anti-order) and rests on emergence/holism (Byrne 1998). A lengthy discussion of what complexity entails and a deciphering of the related scientific terms is not essential here. What is important is the implications this has for social capital: it can only be fully understood by coming to grips with interconnectedness.

If social capital is a network resource, then there is really no option except to see it as relational. Complexity seems useful here because it is founded on the notion of the importance of interconnectedness and non-linearity (Schuller, Baron & Field 2000). The consequence of this is a challenge to those who claim that if social capital is only identified when and if it works, it is tautological, since cause and effect are folded back into each other (Portes 1998; Lin 2001).

I argued earlier that what is needed is a distinction between social capital as a process (cause) and as an outcome (effect). This is not to deny the complexity at the heart of social capital. We have to examine things from different angles simultaneously to capture interactions and changing relationships. A linear view of causation cannot do justice to issues of interconnectedness. The trick is to identify the important components of social capital without following that identification up with a myopic focus on them as independent components. Removing interactions and feedback from the analysis simplifies things, but it ignores the fact that the whole system should be seen as more than a simple aggregation of its component parts.

In science, complexity is a new way of thinking about the collective behaviour of many basic but interacting units. Interactions lead to coherent collective phenomena that can only be described at higher levels than individual units (Coveney & Highfield 1995). Complexity is a result of the patterns of interaction between the elements in a system. In complexity theory as it relates to science, where the components of complex systems are non-human (such as atoms or electronic switches), they have no representational meaning by themselves; they are only meaningful in terms of patterns of relationship with other components (Cilliers 1998). The appropriate focus of attention, then, is clearly connection and relationship, which fits with the social capital framework advocated in this book. With humans involved, the individual components of a system (people) must necessarily be considered too. Translating this into social network terms, it means that while the strength of individual ties between actors is important, it is ultimately the patterning of ties across an entire network that is crucial in determining that network's structure. But to ensure that we do not become too single-minded with this focus on structure, it is also important to keep individual actors in mind. The point here is to use the understanding derived from complexity theory to guide action towards desired outcomes. To do so, David Byrne (1998) argues, means that we have to know a lot and be able to use that knowledge differently. For him, complexity theory offers the possibility of an engaged science, founded in humanity, an awareness of the complexity of the world and a belief that there is something we can do to improve it.

The very notion of complexity throws out a major challenge to governments and to public policy interventions, since much of governing is about simplifying the massive turbulence of events such as the recent global financial meltdown (an example of a complex system) into a few simple policy prescriptions – such as that more regulation of financial services is required. Its usefulness here is mostly metaphorical, providing a rationale for moving beyond an unhelpful level of reduction in order to make sense of the world.

Complexity theory has benefits for thinking about making public policy, if the focus moves from searching for overarching policy prescriptions that are applicable everywhere to identifying policies that might yield great benefits in a particular locale. Indeed, numerous social capital-building policy interventions work at the local level through targeted programs that recognise the need to move beyond viewing health problems, for example, as completely separate from education and housing problems. I return to this later in this chapter.

The link to public policy

Social capital surely has important applications to current problems affecting individuals, communities, organisations and societies. While much has been written on social capital from a variety of disciplinary perspectives, it has largely escaped the scrutiny of the public policy literature, except for uncritical approaches that see an unproblematic link between social capital and a world of good outcomes for citizens, if they will only connect.

In order to move on to the link with public policy, there is a need to briefly discuss how public policy is understood here. There are significant problems with those models of the policy process that attempt to describe it as rational, technical and scientific (Lewis 2005a). First, this approach misses the point of politics. It is better to accept that policy decisions are always political. Second, views of the policy process as sequential and mechanical might well make it understandable, but this conceptualisation leaves out the real complexity of the policy process. As policy making is thoroughly political, it does not neatly conform to a logic of identifying objectives, then finding the best solutions. The policy process is more like a complex system than a simple one. Third, ideas are crucial, because how policy problems are defined generates a list of interested parties and allocates positions of power to them (Stone 2002). The role of ideas is apparent in what might be termed 'the discourse of policy'.

Policy analysis needs to explicitly recognise the political rather than relying on the technical, to think about complex, non-sequential, whole systems rather than the logic of machines, and to understand how ideas are used by actors to shape the policy discourse. Perhaps the best shorthand for this is to state that policy is relational. It is 'the ongoing interactions between people and organisations using structure and argumentation to articulate their ideas' (Lewis 2005a). This clearly fits with the social capital framework proposed in this book, with its foundations in networks and complexity.

The value of social capital in opening up new avenues of exploration, shedding new insights on how we conceive of issues, and strengthening the case for complex and multidimensional investigation is clear. A central point of contention in relation to policy is the state–civil society distinction. Some regard the separation between them as clear cut, but others claim the relationship between them is an ever-changing and symbiotic one. They cannot be disentangled from each other, and 'community' cannot be the panacea for the social ills of modern societies. It bears remembering, when thinking about what policy can do to build social capital, that 'communities are not homogeneous havens of the common good but rather ... need to be fostered and assisted in their social and economic development' (Little 2002: 23). The state cannot be replaced or eradicated. It is in fact needed to provide impetus to stimulate community growth. There is no guarantee that communities or local non-profit groups have the capacity, without state intervention, to expand sufficiently to create the conditions under which social capital can flourish, as some of the contributors to Winter's (2000) book argue.

In working towards a policy framework for social capital, Woolcock (1998) noted, as have others, that social capital has emerged from many different traditions and ideological positions. Social capital has come to be seen as both the infrastructure and the content of social relations, making it impossible to separate what it is from what it does (Edwards & Foley 1998). Most importantly, though, social capital can be used to justify contradictory public policies, even while those all along the political spectrum argue that it is important. On one end of the spectrum, this generates claims from conservatives that the state is not suited to promoting social capital, even though it is able to destroy it. Some go as far as to claim that social capital is enhanced by dismantling the state. At the other end of the spectrum, liberals argue that the state can nurture an environment in which civil society can flourish (Woolcock 1998).

In a comparison of social capital in the US and developing countries and social exclusion in Europe and Latin America (Daly & Silver 2008), the differences between these two concepts and how they reflect the different national and regional contexts they are associated with are explored. In Europe, they claim, the fundamental actors are classes and states, rather than individuals, associations and communities. Of most interest here is the authors' claim that social capital draws out the benefits to be gained by cooperation and participation, and so is focused on consequences, whereas social exclusion is focused on causes. They go on to claim that much of the social capital literature pays little attention to the question of context, while the social exclusion literature sees social exclusion as context specific and focused on maintaining the fabric of social life through obligations to society as a whole, rather than to one's own family or friends.

They end by arguing that both of these concepts have broad appeal, so that many actors mobilise around them. In the case of social capital they claim that the World Bank has used it to deprioritise the role of the state, and that in the US, social capital is generated from within communities, with help from foundations, and policy has had a limited role in producing positive outcomes. They note the danger that this situation could bolster an argument that the state should exit poor communities and leave the problem solving to civil society and individuals. In contrast, they claim that the state is a key actor in the social exclusion framework (Daly & Silver 2008).

Those who have ventured to link social capital to public policy have taken different positions. Some are deeply concerned that connecting the two neither reinvigorates the social nor provides a challenge to the economic view of society, but merely colonises the social with the economic (Fine 1999). Szreter and Woolcock, on the other hand, see the potential for social capital to be used to address issues of power and inequality. In the edited collection of Baron, Field and Schuller (2000), some argue that the state can play a substantial role in creating the conditions for social capital to be built up (Maloney, Smith & Stoker 2000), while others see the need for strong and autonomous civil society to provide a brake on the state (Paterson 2000). Another argument made is that policies that rely on social capital can only operate in concert with strong state interventions (Munn 2000).

In summing up the contributions in their book that deal with the role of the state in social capital, Schuller, Baron and Field see three important dimensions: the need for a devolution downwards of power and responsibility within the state, the need to build links between different policy sectors, and the need to disperse decision making from state to community organisations. As they themselves point out, this is a rather top-down approach to social capital, and it needs to be modified by consideration of the dynamics and power differentials of the situation. Moving responsibility 'down' the chain, or otherwise out of government, raises the potential for governments to divest themselves of responsibility and blame others if things go wrong. This is not to suggest that the state cannot provide leadership, resources and policy settings that encourage social capital. As ever, the devil is in the detail.

Issues of equality and distribution are integral to social capital. What is crucial now is to work out how to use social capital to analyse public policy and to direct new policy making. Schuller, Baron and Field (2000) summarise the promise of social capital as including that: it shifts the focus of analysis from individual actors to the pattern of relations between them; it can act as a link between micro, meso and macro levels of analysis; it is multidisciplinary and interdisciplinary; it reinserts issues of values into social science; and it has heuristic potential. They give most space to the last of these, exploring what analyses result from using social capital as an explanatory variable, and what policy prescriptions flow from them. They noted in 2000 that there had been little of the second of these. Since then there have been various attempts by government to build social capital/inclusion in European countries, and similar initiatives have been implemented in Australia. The thorny question remains: can policy makers intervene from the top down, without going against the principle of bottom-up development that social capital represents, assuming that government cannot determine who we like and who we form friendships with (Perri 6 2004)?

It is social structures, not their consequences, that can be influenced by policy makers. Unless we know the conditions under which social structures generate beneficial outcomes, we cannot orient policy (Durlauf & Fafchamps 2004). This resonates with Woolcock's (1998) point that we should focus on the sources of social capital rather than its consequences, since long-term benefits, if and when they occur, are the result of a combination of many types of social relations, whose relative importance shifts over time.

Numerous grand claims have been made about the benefits of social capital, including that it can reduce transaction costs, facilitate the spread of innovation, promote cooperation in society, yield individual benefits such as health and happiness, and provide savings for economies (Productivity Commission

2003). Putnam (2000) equates social capital with levels of civicness – involvement in associations and participatory behaviour in a community – and argues that civic virtue is on the wane. His pessimistic view of the decline of civil society, and his prescriptions for rebuilding the lost America of earlier times, has led others to argue against the rush to embrace social capital as a form of 'civic elastoplast' (Szreter 2002), or a 'spray on solution' (Bryson & Mowbray 2005). Portes (1998) concludes that there is little ground for the belief that social capital will provide a ready remedy for major social problems.

The problem with social capital being ill defined, vague and multifaceted (Durlauf & Fafchamps 2004) is that this makes it difficult to measure it in meaningful ways, particularly when it can be seen as both a contributor and an outcome. Even in the UK, where it has been heavily promoted, this promotion has been accompanied by a recognition that government interventions to build social capital face significant challenges (UK Cabinet Office 2002).

Social capital theory distinguishes between bonding, bridging and linking ties, but mostly tells us little about network structure or the important nodes and sub-structures. A link is being increasingly claimed between social connectedness and a range of desirable outcomes, such as civic and political engagement, community strength and resilience, health and wellbeing, and knowledge exchange and innovation. Field's (2003) survey of whether social capital does what theorists have claimed reports that there is empirical evidence that supports a strong relationship between social networks and educational performance, that dense networks of firms, researchers and policy makers enable innovation and knowledge exchange, that there is a positive relationship between social capital and health, and that social capital is inversely related to alienation, antisocial behaviour and criminal activity.

However, there is little in the way of ideas about how increased numbers of connections translate into real resources that individuals and collectives use and which public policy could help develop. At the forefront of arguing for the importance of social capital was the Social Exclusion Unit in the UK, which a decade ago claimed that personal social networks that link people together are essential to the functioning of communities and society (Social Exclusion Unit 1999). Vicki Nash (2004) points out the difficulties involved when governments concern themselves in our personal relationships. She also argues, as does Perri 6 (2004), that many policy initiatives have in fact proved detrimental to social relationships, so government should at least try to ensure that it does no harm in terms of social relationships.

The Canadian Government has also been active in generating documents about social capital and its usefulness for policy (Canadian Policy Research Initiative 2003a; 2003b). Nash (2004) claims that there are two scenarios where policy can use social networks as a means for improving things. The first is policy to help particular groups, and is about recommending one type of social network over another. The second is about shaping interactions in particular locations, which she claims is more difficult. These two fit with the cases included in Chapters 5 and 6. Chapter 5, on partnerships, examines a place-based initiative, and Chapter 6, on knowledge, is focused on academics as a specific group. She concludes that it is probably safest to say that policy should support a diversity of ties; this takes us beyond, but not very far beyond, the general claim that government should do no harm.

For policy to be effective, we need to know much more about which networks are valuable in particular circumstances, and be able to evaluate how policy affects them. This throws up a raft of questions about methods for dealing with these kinds of questions. These are central to the discussion in the next section.

Methodological challenges

Much can be said (and indeed has been) about the methodological and measurement challenges that social capital presents. Given the social capital framework presented in this book and the commitment to networks and complexity as a basis for analysis, the most important principle is that any methods used need to be focused on relationships.

Putnam's (2000) composite social capital index is based on a set of indicators of formal and informal networks and social trust. It is made up of measures of community organisational life, engagement in public affairs, community voluntarism, informal sociability and social trust (Schuller, Baron & Field 2000). Much has been written about the inadequacies of the measures used by Putnam, who taps only a very narrow meso-level definition of social capital (Halpern 2005). A very simple measure of social trust which has been used extensively is the

World Values Survey question which asks: 'Generally speaking, would you say that most people can be trusted or that you can't be too careful in dealing with people?' This has been used in many nations and been shown to be strongly correlated with the kind of measure that Putnam uses. This does not qualify it as a good way to measure social capital. It is simply a measure of social trust at a generalised level (national/regional/community).

The Australian Bureau of Statistics' (ABS) attempts to map out the concept in order to measure it rest on a Putnamesque division into networks, norms and trust (ABS 2004). The emphasis on these is not surprising, given that the ABS is conducting large-scale surveys. But social capital has many levels and forms and cannot be captured in a single metric that covers just one dimension on one level. It is difficult to collect relational data with sample surveying, because those surveyed are unlikely to be connected to each other, which means that no reciprocal tie data is available. A census approach is required to collect network tie data, which is why so many social network studies deal with captive groups in schools and organisations. General sampling methods pose problems if social capital is a network-based concept best measured via relational data.

Since relationships are the foundation of social capital, it follows that relationships should be the focus of understanding and measurement. While the social capital theories focused on here are individual-based, they are also network-based, and interested in quality as well as quantity of network ties. Trying to use networks in social surveys that aim to make claims about social capital has led to a reductionist approach, and survey questions about, for example, how many people you know. While network size is probably important, it seems unlikely that more is always better. If you know lots of people but you don't believe that any of them would actually help you when you needed help, then this network is not in fact a positive for you.

Social capital is based on relationships, so the quality or strength of those relationships is clearly important. Not all network ties are equally important and their importance can vary between situations. That is, one contact might be highly valued in regard to the advice they can provide, but of little use in being able to provide economic support. Of course, some ties are used for many purposes (multiplexity), and once a connection is established for one purpose it is not uncommon that it is then used for others. But there is not a one-to-one correspondence between ties of different strengths for different purposes. This is what has led a number of scholars to claim that social network analysis represents the way forward in measuring social capital (see Perri 6 2004; Nash 2004; Daly & Silver 2008).

Social network-based attempts to measure social capital have generally used either name generators or position generators. Name generators ask individuals to list people they are close to or could call upon for help in a particular situation (for examples, see Wellman 1979; Burt 1984). Position generators ask individuals for information on who they know in certain positions, such as doctors, teachers, politicians. Nan Lin initiated this approach, so it's not surprising that the focus is on measuring access to resources through people in different occupations (see Lin & Dumin 1986).

Martin Van der Gaag and Tom Snijders (2005) pointed out the shortcomings of name generators, which yield no information on the likelihood of the nominated people being able to generate access to resources, and of position generators, which assume that people in certain positions provide access to social capital when it may in fact be simply access to capital. They created instead a resource generator, which asks individuals who they know who could provide them with access to resources (such as helping repair a bike), and who they would discuss intimate matters with. This represents one of the best attempts to measure social capital as a multidimensional and network-based concept.

Durlauf and Fafchamps (2004), at the end of their extensive review of social capital, conclude that the most successful theoretical work on social capital is that which models it as a form of social network structure and uses the presence of that structure to understand how individual outcomes are affected. They note that the role of networks in facilitating exchange is one of the most compelling findings in the social capital literature. Likewise, Daly and Silver (2008) argue that a focus on social networks is important in advancing scholarship on social capital. They claim that data on the composition of social networks is needed to allow for analysis of different forms of capital and different levels of those forms. They also note the large array of social network analysis concepts that are likely to be helpful, but warn that qualitative data on networks is also required, as a structural approach might miss the substance, intentions, and historical and cultural context of social relations.

Social network analysis is based on analysing the relationships among entities, and the patterns and implications of these. One of its most important assumptions is that observations are not independent – which is the foundation underpinning standard statistical analysis. Instead, data is relational, based on connections that tie actors to each other. Hence observations cannot be reduced to properties of individual actors, as this negates their relational nature. If social capital is not an attribute of individuals but a function of the relationships between them, then social network analysis is clearly an appropriate means for framing the questions to be asked and the means for analysing the responses. Social network analysis, which deals with relational data, has many terms and concepts that overlap with those of social capital, and its approaches and techniques have been increasingly applied to studies of social capital. It is at the individual level where the most appropriate methods have been developed.

Mapping social networks of interpersonal ties allows the analyst to generate a detailed picture of individual connections. By examining who is connected to whom, it is possible to see who has access to resources and who occupies strategic positions within a network. Networks can be based on any number of (instrumental and expressive) relationships. There is no need to make any assumptions beyond that people are in contact with others for a variety of reasons. However, these concepts are not as yet widely understood by academics or policy makers or the general public. This makes them difficult to comprehend in the face of the more usual survey data, with its more familiar terminology and procedures. The newer concepts and approaches can be learnt, of course, but it will be some time before there is a large cohort of people who are educated in this new but expanding field.

Social network analysis and its emphasis on structure can lead to the idea of agency being ignored. Bob Jessop's (2000) strategic-relational approach encourages the analyst to examine structure in relation to action and action in relation to structure. Combining network analysis with descriptive narratives, both of which are based on the observations of individuals, brings the actors back in. Structural and discursive approaches have been combined where possible in the empirical cases presented in this book. I first described this approach in an article (Lewis 2005b) that argued for combining social network analysis with a more open exploration of how participants in a network understand it (what some call seeing the network twice).

In the four cases in Chapters 3 to 6, a number of social network concepts are used. An overview is provided in the next section, and more details can be found in each chapter. Greater detail about social network analysis and the concepts and measures used in these chapters can be found in texts on the subject (see, for example, Wasserman & Faust 1994; Degene & Forse 1999; Scott 2000), and on the International Network for Social Network Analysis (INSNA) website (http://www.insna.org/). The approach examines social networks as a set of connections, as well as a narrative about what those connections are used for and how they are valued. This provides information on the pattern of connections between people for various purposes (social structure) along with information about how people use and value those connections (agency).

Influence, innovation, partnerships and knowledge

There are significant challenges in turning the concept of social capital into something that can be measured in a manner that does not revert to the extremes of generality and reductionism. This chapter and the previous one outlined some of those challenges, and suggested a set of principles for social capital that, if followed, should lead to an ongoing interplay between theory and empirical research which will improve the foundations of the concept and generate better approaches and methods for measuring it. There are also challenges in converting social connectedness research into something that can be useful for public policy. When governments include social capital on the agenda, a host of questions are raised about what kind of policy interventions should be pursued if the goal is to increase social connectedness. There are also some major questions about the boundaries of what government should do and what should be left to others, either because government cannot play a role or because it is better if others do.

The framework for social capital outlined at the beginning of this chapter brings together existing knowledge of the types and features of networks that facilitate connectedness in order to devise a strong policy approach. Knowledge about social capital has been developed in diverse, yet related, bodies of theory, and has rarely been applied clearly to issues of policy and governance. Discussions of social capital and public policy need to explicate the effects of both the quality and positionality of links within different social networks. Once this has been achieved, there is real potential to link the roles of policy making and governance in building social capital.

Four different cases are examined in the following four chapters. Two of these are about social connectedness and the public policy process (Chapters 3 and 4). They are stories of individuals occupying important network positions, from which they are able to exercise influence in making public policy, either in setting the agenda or in innovating. The first deals with a social network of influence in the policy process and how it shapes the policy agenda. It demonstrates how network positions are related to an actor's ability to influence what is regarded as important for policy attention. The second examines innovation within governments, as a particular form of the achievement of policy. It examines networks of advice seeking and information searching inside governments, and assesses the importance of these in signalling who the innovators are.

Chapter 3, on influence, employs an analysis of structural equivalence, which looks for actors who have similar patterns of connections. It also uses in-degree centrality to demonstrate who the most influential actors are, and betweenness centrality to find who is bridging across disconnected parts of the network. Finally, it links network position (in terms of centrality) with issues, to see whether those who are close to the centre of power are interested in the issues that are most widely seen to be important. This is a network based on who is seen to be influential.

Chapter 4, on innovation, also uses in-degree centrality, but this time in relation to levels in the hierarchy and roles, rather than in relation to individuals. This generates an analysis of which positions are important. It also looks at the ego networks (all the direct ties to and from an actor) of key individuals in different governments, to see how connected the two arms of government – political and administrative – are. Multiple regression using individual centrality scores shows the importance of networks overall. Advice and strategic information networks are considered in this chapter.

The second two cases (Chapters 5 and 6) relate to the use of public policy to build social capital. They are stories of government intervening through policy measures that help join things up between organisations and individuals in order to achieve desired outcomes. The first of these relates to two different kinds of partnerships, one of which was introduced to improve service coordination in primary healthcare, and the other of which was introduced to help build communities in areas of disadvantage. The final case is about policies that encourage collaboration between academics, in order to pool resources, contribute to the production of new knowledge and increase publishing.

Chapter 5, on partnerships, uses in-degree centrality as a way to assess the importance of individuals. It also uses centrality measures for people in the same agency, to gauge how important certain organisations are. Network maps are used to show the crucial role being played by brokers in these networks, and also to show how the position of actors changes over time. The networks of interest are based on day-to-day work contact and getting strategic information.

Chapter 6, on knowledge, uses maps to demonstrate the larger context and patterns of interaction in research. Ego-based analyses focus on a number of different proximity measures of ties. The networks in this case are the concrete networks of who publishes together, and the more expressive networks, which are based on shared research interests and discussions.

These four empirically grounded chapters demonstrate how social capital affects the making of public policy, and how public policy making affects social capital. The book's conclusion brings together insights from the cases to illuminate the structure and quality of networks of different types, points to how these translate into action, and highlights the actions that appear to support access to embedded resources. Drawing lessons from the four case studies, it demonstrates how social capital can help in understanding the policy process, and what policy can and should do to build social capital.

3 Influence

Understanding how the policy agenda is structured is a field of political analysis that has been around for a long time. Community power studies, studies of insiders and outsiders, attempts to map out the visible face of power, and concerns with uncovering the invisible face of power, reached a peak in the 1970s, and then interest moved on. It is difficult to get a firm grip on who wields the greatest ability to shape the policy agenda through power studies – we can never be sure that we have really got to the bottom of who is influential. But what if we were to recast this as a social capital and public policy story, one that has a focus on not only who has influence but also who is connected to whom?

Policy influence in terms of social capital is a story of self-organising networks. The core concern is with the connections that arise through opportunistic meetings or structured interactions, and which might then translate into ongoing links between individuals who are in a position to influence policy, and become even more able to influence policy through these links. To be sure, many of the people of influence in particular policy settings hold positions of power that grant them opportunities to exercise power. The heads of important organisations, ministers and their advisers, and high-ranking bureaucrats are obvious contenders. But additional access to resources is generated through the interpersonal connections that underpin the formation of sub-groups of actors. We can postulate, using what we know about network theories, that those who are proximate in network terms might also be similar and be interested in pursuing similar agenda items. This is what this chapter focuses on.

The network characteristics which are most likely to be useful in explaining social capital in policy making relate to network substructures. We want to be able to observe groups who are tightly interconnected, and to see what they have in common. In power terms, it is also useful to see which individuals are located in strategically important network positions. Centrality is a clear marker of who has visible or positional power, while betweenness signals those who are less visible but can play valuable linking roles. Both are important. And we are of course also interested in mapping associations between network positions and policy issues, to see whether those who have similar sets of issues are located close to each other.

This leads into the outcomes question. How do these informal networks relate to the overall policy agenda? Actors are engaged in particular policy fields because they want to achieve something. John Kingdon (1995) suggested a range of motivations for being what he calls a policy entrepreneur, from being passionate about getting a particular issue onto the change agenda through to a pure enjoyment of the cut and thrust of politics. It can be difficult to impute these motivations, but here they are not crucial – it is the issues they are promoting and their links to others with similar interests that are the important things to examine.

The social capital framework provided in this book gives a new perspective on this old topic of influence and agenda setting. It draws attention to interactions at the micro level that create embedded resources outside the formal institutions of policy and service delivery, and that might have large effects on what is the (collective) focus of governmental attention. In other words, this approach to examining power adds a novel way of observing it through individuals, which adds a new dimension to the more macro-level approaches (which focus on systems) and meso-level approaches (which deal with organisations).

This chapter is the strongest example in this book of why it makes more sense to begin from a rational choice perspective in thinking about social capital. The individuals involved are not necessarily operating in a space of trust and shared norms – in fact it can be quite the opposite. Yet longevity and a shared history in a policy sector generate enduring connections. Gains can be made by distinguishing between ties and the actual effects in policy agenda-setting terms, but causality flows in both directions: individuals with influence have agenda-setting potential, and their links with others reinforce their influence on the agenda. As in all the cases in this book, the importance of patterns of connectedness is clear. The network concepts used in this case are structural equivalence, in-degree centrality, betweenness centrality and proximity.

There is almost no literature that uses social capital theories to examine influence in public policy. Before proceeding to a consideration of how the social capital framework of this book helps in this case, some background on influence in policy making is provided.

Influence and agenda setting

Policy making is fundamentally shaped by actors who seek to use the resources at their disposal to have their concerns taken seriously. The making of public policy rests on the accumulation and use of power by those involved in the policy process. But examining this is far from straightforward, even when power is used transparently. A number of approaches at different levels have been used to understand power and policy making in the health sector. At the macro level, Robert Alford's (1975) work on the dominant, challenging and repressed structural interests that shape health policy alerts us to existing social, political and economic structures. In Alford's classification, professional monopolists are the dominant group, and it is therefore their interests that are served by existing structures. Corporate rationalists challenge these dominant interests, by emphasising rational planning and efficiency ahead of deference to the expertise of medical professionals. Equal health advocates represent the repressed structural interests, and push for better access to services (and so against the entrenched structures).

This, and other macro-level explanations, reveals only part of the story of policy influence. Focusing on connections between individuals makes these relationships central to understanding policy influence at another level. Looking at individuals rather than societal structures opens up a space outside the long-established descriptions that go hand in hand with examinations of powerful interests. Using social capital to conceptualise and examine influence in the policy process promises new insights on how the resources embedded in a policy sector are used to set the policy agenda.

This case provides a prime example of the important assumption made earlier, that to be linked into a particular network does not automatically indicate like-mindedness or trust between actors. There are relationships, but these relationships are not necessarily agreeable or used for the common good. Connections provide access to resources and control within a network. The connections might be based on shared values, but they can equally be based on competition or obligation.

Also important to this particular case is the distinction between personal, positional and social resources described in Chapter 1. Personal resources (human capital) are those fully owned by an actor, such as gender and education. Positional resources are vested in a position; they grant an actor resources while in that position, but they remain attached to the position (for example, the level in a hierarchy, or the prestige of an organisation) when the incumbent moves on. Social resources are based on relationships with others which, once created, can be appropriated for other uses. So people you knew at school or university can become friends who might provide access to valuable resources if they move into important positions.

In Chapter 1, the concepts of homophily and heterophily were discussed as important organising principles for the patterning of resource linkages in networks. These too are important here. Homophilous ties are more frequent, easy to make and keep, and are used to maintain existing resources. Heterophilous ties, which are less frequent and take more energy, provide the biggest gains by providing access to additional and different resources.

Using a social capital framework which allows that networks have an impact on shaping the policy agenda offers a different way to observe the process by which issues make it from the long list of things that are swirling around in the 'policy primeval soup' (Kingdon 1995) to the short list of issues that are the subject of serious policy attention. Examining policy influence as an instance of social capital at work is a novel way of thinking about which individuals have power through their networks as well as their formal positions, and how they shape the policy agenda and allow or stop policy change.

This case is a study of networks of influence in health policy in Victoria. The study is made up of a survey in 2001, which was reported in Lewis (2005b) and Lewis (2006), and a follow-up survey in 2004, which has not previously been published. These two surveys together highlight changes over time, providing insights into the dynamics of policy agenda setting.

Mapping influence requires the identification of influential actors. Positional methods for doing this define influential actors as those holding positions in the top levels of business, government and unions (Kadushin 1968; Laumann & Knoke 1987). This method leads to important community groups or individuals being overlooked. Reputational methods, in contrast, use elites to nominate others whom they consider influential. This can lead to the nomination of influential friends, neighbours, people they like, or those who are merely noisy (Hawley & Svara 1972).

Perceptions of influence among elites was the focus, so a reputational approach was used. This process is known as a name generator in social network analysis, and is widely used (see, for example, Burt 1984). Rather than selecting someone in an obviously important position to begin the snowball (such as the current health minister), an academic was chosen as the starting point. This initial actor was not medically qualified, but was heavily involved in the health sector in Victoria as well as across Australia. Since medically qualified individuals will be numerous (Lewis & Considine 1999), and assuming that many ties will be homophilous, it was important to start 'outside' medicine.

In mid 2001, this actor was asked to nominate those regarded as influential, using the following definition:

> influence is defined as a demonstrated capacity to do one or more of the following: shape ideas about policy, initiate policy proposals, substantially change or veto others' proposals, or substantially affect the implementation of policy in relation to health. Influential people are those who make a significant difference at one or more stages of the policy process (Lewis 2006: 2129).

Everyone nominated was then contacted and asked to make their own list, using the same definition. They were not provided with others' lists. New nominees were then approached and asked to do the same. No set number of nominations was asked for, as specifying a certain number was considered to risk either eliminating important people, or forcing people to keep adding others who they in fact thought were not especially influential.

In this type of network there is in effect no boundary. An empirical approach was taken in the study, with the boundary defined by nominations. A decision was made to stop after five rounds.[1] This generated 218 names, 115 of whom were contacted. Initially everybody nominated was approached, but after the snowballing was stopped, only those nominated more than twice were contacted. At the end of this, 62 of the 115 people contacted (54 per cent) had returned nominations of influence, noting whether they had ongoing contact with those they nominated.

This procedure for identifying influential actors generates a picture of a particular locale within a network around the starting point. That is, the resultant sub-graph of the network identified is not necessarily representative of the 'whole' network (which effectively has no boundary). A different starting point could generate a substantially different map. However, most of the actors identified hold positions of influence in the health sector. This indicates that the resultant network has validity. So while this map does not give the topography of an entire network, it certainly yields the contours of perceived influence in this locale.

Based on these nominations of 218 influential actors, those who top the list are health academics, senior bureaucrats and people located in research institutes and NGOs. Most of the influential actors are medically trained, and the vast majority of them are men. This describes what are essentially votes of perceived influence, but reveals nothing about the relationship between those actors.

Network structure

The information generated by asking people to nominate who they saw as having influence provided relational data. This was used to examine the structure of the network.[2] For social network analysis, it is important to have both ties sent (nominations of others) and ties received (nominations from others). In this study, two senior bureaucrats within the state health authority received the second and eighth highest number of nominations. However, neither of these people returned forms themselves and so were excluded from the network analysis. This is unlikely to have greatly affected the study overall, given their positions and likely connections to many of those who were nominated by others.

The information collected through the nomination process included whether the nominators had ongoing contact with those they nominated. The majority of ties (82 per cent) were to actors the nominator claimed to have ongoing contact with, and another 15 per cent were to people they had met. These people appear to have based their judgments of influence on who they know personally. However, actors holding the positions regarded as influential sit on many committees and boards together and have been around the health sector for a long time (see Lewis 2006), so they will know other influential actors. Perhaps the tendency to nominate known others indicates homophily or a tendency to claim acquaintance with influential people in order to demonstrate their own influence by association. But the more likely explanation seems to be that they have ongoing contact or have at least met most of the other actors who are seen to be influential. Since virtually all ties were of the same type (that is, people the nominator knew personally), the remaining discussion is based simply on whether ties are present or absent.

An important network concept here is structural equivalence. This relates to the concept of social position, and is based on the idea that people within a network might be connected to completely different sets of individuals, but can be seen as equivalent in structural terms if the patterns of relations they have with others are similar. Blockmodelling partitions actors into structurally equivalent sets within a network, based on regularities of patterns of relations among actors (Breiger 1976). This means establishing which actors nominate others in the network in a similar pattern, and which actors are themselves nominated by others in similar patterns. The resulting model is a view of social structure obtained by aggregating relational data without imposing *a priori* categories or attributes of actors (White, Boorman & Breiger 1976).

Network structure, based on the data gathered for this study, was analysed as a blockmodel. This generated the eight blocks shown in Table 3.1. The labels (names of blocks) reflect an assessment of what the individuals within each block have in common. The numbers in Table 3.1 indicate the proportions of ties between the blocks. Hence, 0.44 (or 44 per cent) of the total possible ties going from the Hospitals and La Trobe University block to the Core influentials block were present. Only two of the eight blocks were relatively cohesive as measured by the proportion of ties within a block (on the diagonal): Public health medicine is the most cohesive block, with 40 per cent of ties internal, followed by the Core block, with 23 per cent of ties internal.

Table 3.1 Influence network blocks 2001*

Block (number in block)	1	2	3	4	5	6	7	8
1. Core influentials (8)	.23							
2. Defined areas (4)								
3. Hospitals and La Trobe (9)	.44							
4. Consumer and legal (4)				.39				
5. Public health medicine (9)	.38				.40			
6. Particular diseases/communities (8)	.20				.24			
7. Monash University associated (12)	.25				.32			
8. Peripheral but connected (8)	.34				.31			

* Only proportions of .20 and greater are shown for ease of interpretation.

The Core block contains actors widely seen by others in the network as influential, who themselves nominated few people as influential – especially outside this core group. It has eight people in highly visible positions: the Minister for Health; the Minister's Chief of Staff; the Secretary of the Department of Human

Influence • 87

Services (DHS); the Secretary of the Australian Nursing Federation (Victorian Branch); two deans; and two others. The second block consists of actors who listed others only within their own defined areas, who were not nominated by anybody else.

The third block is people located in either public teaching hospitals or La Trobe University.[3] The fourth contains people with a consumer and/or legal focus. The fifth consists of actors located in various universities, research institutes and health-related NGOs. Their commonality seems to be their interest in communities, populations, health promotion and disease prevention rather than individual and curative care. All of the actors in this block had medical qualifications.[4] The sixth block is people interested in particular diseases or communities (such as HIV/AIDS or Aboriginal people), and the seventh is people with current or previous associations with Monash University. The final block is termed 'peripheral' because these actors nominated highly influential people but were not recognised as very influential themselves.

A diagram of this network structure is shown in Figure 3.1. The lines between the groups have different thicknesses, based on the proportion of possible ties shown in Table 3.1. The size of the circles varies according to the mean number of votes per person in that block, ranging from a mean of 17.5 for those in the Core group, down to 2.3 for Defined areas. The Core block is centrally positioned in this network, as the arrowheads pointing towards it indicate. It contains actors who were nominated by people in all the other blocks except the Defined areas and Consumer and legal. The Public health medicine block is the next most central.

Figure 3.1 Network of influence in health 2001

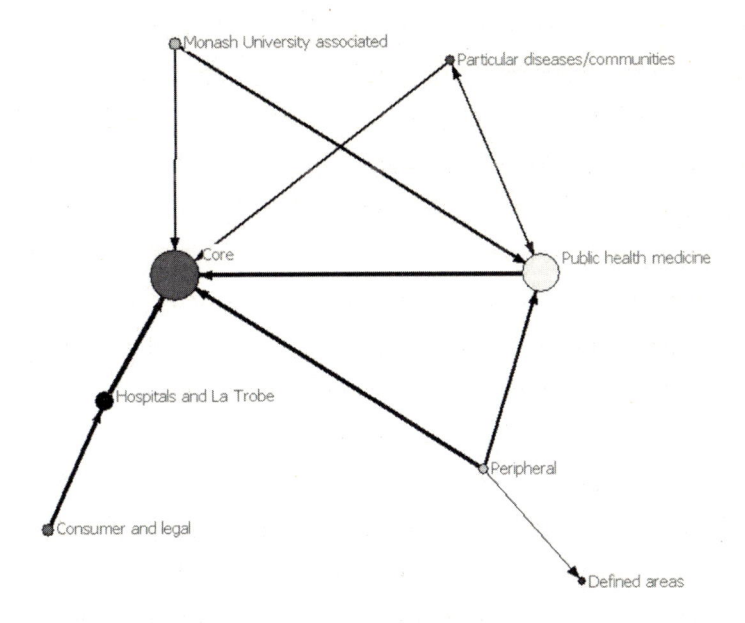

This examination of structural equivalence indicates that there is a core group: actors in key positions who are both structurally important and highly visible in health policy in Victoria. This is not surprising and it seems reasonable to assume that whoever occupied the positions would be widely regarded as influential. The other most central group, Public health medicine, is more interesting, because it is a less obviously influential group of people at first glance. These actors are located in universities, research institutes and NGOs, all are medically trained, and eight of the nine are men. This is also the most cohesive group, which suggests that these ties are homophilous, connecting like to like.

Influence • 89

Influential individuals

The actors in the Core and Public health medicine groups are clearly in the best position to affect health policy. Those in other groups must find a way to connect in order to wield influence. However, structural equivalence in network terms does not imply that everybody within a block is equally influential. Measuring centrality is a way of determining who the most important individuals within a network are. A different approach was taken to describing influence. Interviews were conducted with 20 of these influential people (14 men and 6 women).[5] They were asked to discuss: what they currently regarded as the most important issues in health policy; who they worked with in relation to these or other issues; and who they had links with more generally. The interviews were tape recorded and transcribed, and quotes are used to highlight different types of connectedness, and their perceptions of the network and their positions within it.

Table 3.2 contains two measures of centrality for the 12 most central actors in this network. The in-degree centrality of an actor indicates the extent to which other actors chose this person as influential. It is the number of ties received by an actor, and hence a measure of the extent to which others see an individual as having important resources. Actors with high in-degree centrality scores are more highly connected and also more highly recognised as having influence of some kind. The table lists actors in rank order of their in-degree centrality. The second measure, of betweenness centrality, indicates the strategic importance of an actor within a network. Betweenness is defined as the number of single ties that connect a person to sub-groups of actors (Krackhardt 1992). It measures the extent to which an actor has the potential to play a broker or intermediary role within a network. High betweenness means an actor is in a position to act as a gatekeeper or bridge for information flow through a network, by linking up actors who are otherwise not connected.

Table 3.2 Centrality of individuals 2001*

	Centrality In-degree	Centrality Betweenness
Dean of Health Sciences, La Trobe University	34	6.6
Minister for Health	28	7.1
Dean of Medicine, Monash University	28	26.2
Dean of Medicine, University of Melbourne	25	1.8
CEO of VicHealth	25	15.9
CEO of Bayside Health	20	12.7
Secretary, Department of Human Services	17	0.4
Chief Health Officer, Department of Human Services	16	3.9
Director, Cancer Council of Victoria	12	5.0
Director, Monash Institute of Health Services Research	12	9.1
Minister's Chief of Staff	12	0.4
Secretary Australian Nursing Federation (Vic)	12	1.4

* Those included had an in-degree centrality score of 12 or more.

Five of these most central actors are academics (including three deans), two are senior bureaucrats, one is the CEO of a public hospital group, and one is the CEO of VicHealth.[6] The Minister for Health, the Minister's Chief of Staff and the head of the state branch of the nursing union make up the rest. The deans head up the in-degree centrality list, along with the Minister. The following quote neatly captures a picture of the resources that one of the deans was able to access through his formal position:

> As a dean I talk to my fellow colleagues as deans. We talk to the Commonwealth. The deans meet with the Commonwealth Health and Aged Care group ... As a dean I get access to the Minister and senior people in DHS [Department of Human Services] and talk to them about these problems.

Another actor described more of a personal network view:

> I know the *Age* [newspaper] journalists reasonably well; they use me as a sounding board ... I have reasonably good access to Thwaites [the Minister] ... in the minister's office AA is a friend ... [O]f the ministerial advisers, one of them used to work for me ..., in the department BB I know, CC I know and get on reasonably well with.

The pattern of intermediary influence is somewhat different. One of the deans of medicine, a hospital CEO and the CEO of VicHealth have the highest scores, making them the best positioned to act in linking roles in the network. One interviewee with a high betweenness centrality score remarked: '[T]his is contact city. I mean, we're just in the middle of lots of things, so if people are interested in doing those sorts of things then this can be a networker's paradise.' Those in structurally important positions, such as the top health bureaucrat, the top political adviser and the top nursing union official all have reasonably high recognition as influential, but low betweenness centrality.

Finally, being associated with a policy area for a long time appears to increase the chances of being regarded as influential. This is related to the notion of preferential attachment in networks. Network growth (the arrival of new actors) does not occur randomly: new attachments are made to those nodes that have been around longer, and to those that are popular (Barabasi 2002). Comments by core influentials about their longevity in and knowledge of the area highlight the importance of this: 'I know how the system works; I know a lot of the players in the system so that's been a huge benefit.'

In this network, those most widely regarded as influential are academics, medically qualified and male. Positional actors (the top politician, political adviser and bureaucrat in health and the top nursing official) form part of a core group within this network structure. A second central group consists of people working in academia, research institutes and health-related NGOs. Medical academics appear to combine positional and personal influence, and play significant intermediary roles across the network.

This structural analysis points to the importance of individuals with medical qualifications located throughout the network. They are strongly connected to other medical (mostly) men, which provides them with powerful connections through their formal positions, and ensures that their concerns are embedded in the network through homophilous ties.

This analysis yields a detailed picture of perceived influence as social capital. It uncovers patterns that indicate which groups of actors are regarded as the most influential in policy making, and helps unpack their inherent personal and positional resources, as well as those based on social ties. While some core positions are important, actors with more enduring and informal connections based on shared attributes and longevity in a sector provide the linkages that help to hold the network together.

Using social capital as a basis for analysing policy influence is a novel approach, both because it overturns the more usual ways of thinking about social capital at the collective level, and because it sees policy making as an endeavour that rests on relationships. It reveals which individuals have power by virtue of their position in relation to other actors in their network. They are very aware of their own positions in the network, and their own perceptions of where they sit, as described in the interviews, reflected their centrality and their intermediary roles.

Having identified who is influential, and who is connected to whom, the next section examines individuals and their ideas about problems and potential solutions. It moves away from the structural side of the story, to explain how networks shape policy agendas.

The policy agenda

In policy agenda setting, some claim that agenda items will come from outside government and from a wide array of groups, reaching the agenda through the mobilisation of the relevant groups by political leaders (Cobb & Elder 1971). Others propose that there is a kind of closed shop inside government setting the agenda through the circulation of ideas within professional circles and policy elites (Walker 1969). A compromise is to claim a coincidence of inside and outside interests that contribute to agenda setting, or that agenda items are added or removed through changes in political party control or internal party balances, brought about by elections (Brady 1982).

Networks add to this topic an examination of the links between individual actors, their positions in a network, and the meanings that tie them to each other (White 1992). Actors are inextricably interlinked on the basis of formal connections within and between organisations, as well as through other more informal links. Some actors also share concerns about particular issues. Issues seem likely to travel through networks based on which actors are proximate. The connections between actors will change as people become interested in different issues.

To understand setting the policy agenda as related to social capital is to understand that connections between actors can be based on this shared interest in particular policy issues. The policy issue network literature suggests that policy can be viewed as a set of recurring interactions between actors within policy fields (Skok 1995). Issue networks can mean tightly structured systems (or sub-governments), or more open and amorphous groups. These policy networks or advocacy coalitions or policy communities are not the central point here. We want to locate which actors in a policy network share a concern about a particular issue, recognising that a network member might be interested in a number of different issues at any time.

Table 3.3 Most important issues and difficult issues in 2001

Issue in health policy	Important issues	Difficult issues	Total
1. Inequalities in health/structural determinants	4	7	11
2. Recruitment and retention of health workforce/ training and planning issues	7	2	9
3. Demand in public hospitals	7	1	8
4. Split responsibilities in the health system (disaggregation, fragmentation, levels of government)	7	1	8
5. Lack of emphasis on prevention, health promotion, public health/focus on acute care	4	3	7
6. Improving the quality of care	6	1	7
Managing within revenue constraints/ competing priorities outside health	5	0	5
Turning research into policy/ evidence-based policy/practice	5	0	5
Lack of physical activity, poor nutrition, illicit drugs, tobacco control	3	2	5
Increasing medical/biotech research investment in Victoria	2	2	4
Increasing research, education, training, leadership in public health	2	2	4
Access to care for disadvantaged groups	3	0	3
Ageing and chronic illness	2	1	3
Getting more consumer and carer involvement/dialogue	2	1	3
Mental health	2	1	3
Getting more emphasis on primary care, moving away from GPs and hospitals	2	1	3

Problems caused by market/competition, including concerns other than effectiveness	2	1	3
Managing community expectations/budget not unlimited	1	2	3
Indigenous health	0	3	3
Whole of government approach to health needed	2	0	2
Food safety, immunisation	2	0	2
Increasing costs of pharmaceuticals, technologies	0	2	2
Inefficient distribution of resources	1	0	1
Rural health	1	0	1
Medical litigation system	1	0	1
Total	73	33	106

The influential actors interviewed in the second part of the study of influence were asked to nominate the issues they currently saw as the most important in health policy (see Lewis 2005b for more details). This allowed an unprompted version of important issues to be constructed. A set number of issues was not specified, but a maximum of five was suggested. To identify 'difficult' policy issues, interviewees were also asked about important issues where they thought no change had occurred, either because the issue was too difficult or because it had been tackled ineffectively. Table 3.3 shows all the issues, rank ordered from the most frequently nominated to the least frequently nominated.[7]

The issues seen to be important by the largest number of interviewees were problems in the recruitment and retention of the health workforce, the demand for public hospital services, and the split responsibilities in the Australian health system, each nominated by seven interviewees as important. The need to improve the quality of care was described as important by six people. Inequalities in health or the structural determinants of health, and a lack of effort in prevention of illness and/or an overemphasis on acute (hospital) care, were both nominated as important by four interviewees.

Of the issues seen as not being dealt with, or as being tackled ineffectively, the most frequently chosen were inequalities in health, with seven nominations, followed by a lack of effort in prevention and indigenous health, with three nominations each. By their nature, these are complicated policy agenda items that do not fit neatly into curative healthcare. It is not surprising then that these were the most often nominated when the emphasis was on issues where change was difficult.

A clear distinction arose in the interviews between the issues that were most often described in terms of actions being taken to fix them, and the issues that were more often seen as difficult and discussed as the issues that nobody really knows what to do about, or the issues that people are not seriously doing anything about. The important/difficult distinction was very clear, both in terms of whether an issue was nominated as important or difficult, and in terms of how the issue was spoken about.

Some quotes from the interviews give a flavour of how the different types of issues were discussed. The first is from someone in the core group, describing an important issue with high political sensitivity:

Obviously I think access to acute healthcare services is

politically very important and that's got a range of sub-issues, the emergency demand and waiting lists and ... all of those sorts of things.

The second is from someone describing a difficult issue:

[O]ne of the biggest things that comes out of that arena is the inequalities in health status across the community and geography of Victoria ... and how to target what needs to be done ... how do we shift resources and invest in this very tight constrained budget, efforts around these kinds of things?

Issues and influential actors

Using the information collected about who is perceived to have influence and what they see as the most important issues, it is possible to examine the correspondence between the level of influence and the salience of issues. In-degree centrality is used as the measure of influence, as reported earlier in this chapter. The degree of salience of an issue is based on how many of the 20 interviewees nominated it.

The most influential actors chose access to public hospitals, split responsibilities in the health system, and workforce recruitment and retention. In contrast, lack of emphasis on prevention, health inequalities, and improving the quality of care were chosen by only a single individual ranked in the top five. Prevention and health inequalities were nominated by those further down the ranking. This analysis demonstrates an association between those most highly ranked and the most frequently nominated issues.

Another way of looking at this is to consider whose list of

issues had the closest correspondence with the overall view of which issues were the most important. There is a strong concordance between influence and issues. The list of issues mentioned was wide ranging, but those widely seen as influential had at least a couple of the most salient issues on their lists.

Linking actors and their concerns in a network structure makes it possible to see the policy agenda as a product of the connections between actors. And conversely, by highlighting which issues are seen to be important by which influential actors, the structuring of connectedness based on common concerns can be observed.

Clearly, where you sit in the network has a significant effect on what you think the main issues are, and what's important, suggesting that these networks do shape the policy agenda to a significant extent. Analysing network structures alongside who is discussing particular issues sheds light on the link between network position and the distribution of issues. This provides an example of social capital at work in the policy process, as it appears that the interconnections between actors correspond to agreed issue sets. Those who are more central are focused on the issues that top the policy agenda, and those who are close to each other in network terms regard the same issues as important.

Dynamics and changing the agenda

A repeat of the 2001 study in 2004 sheds some light on the dynamics of this network of influence. Following the same methods and using the same person as the starting point, it generated a new network of influence based on responses from 53 people, followed by interviews with 18 actors across the network. An examination of structural equivalence was again carried out using the blockmodelling procedure, and the results are provided in Table 3.4. The most highly nominated group of people contains the Secretary of the Department, the Minister's chief of staff, two hospital CEOs, a dean and the CEO of VicHealth (who was in the Public health medicine block in the analysis for 2001). This is the Core group in 2004, and the (different) Minister does not appear because she did not participate. The second block is a group of people who worked in state government departments other than DHS, and included an academic with a strong interest in health systems and one Federal politician. This group has been labelled State government – financing.

The third block consists of nine people who worked in hospitals and represented medical and nursing professional organisations, and two nursing academics, and is called Workforce and hospitals. The fourth block was the second group that included several state government officials, but in this case they were from DHS, and it also included one of the junior Ministers (within the human services portfolio) and two public health academics. This is called State government – health. The fifth group is similar to the Public health medicine group from 2001, and includes academics in public health departments and heads of a number of disease prevention and health promotion NGOs. They are not all medically qualified this time, so are termed Public health. The sixth group is people who deal with specific communities or client groups and have a strong prevention focus, so are called Community based. The seventh block is a collection of people

Influence • 101

who are all in some way related to cancer prevention and treatment, and most of them are in advocacy and support positions, so this group is called Cancer advocacy. The final group consists of three people without much in common who are not strongly connected to the rest of the network, so have been termed Peripheral.

Table 3.4 Influence network blocks 2004*

Block (number in block)	1	2	3	4	5	6	7	8
1. Core influentials (6)	.43							
2. State government – financing (8)								
3. Workforce and hospitals (9)	.22							
4. State government – health (9)	.56							
5. Public health (8)	.23				.21			
6. Community based (6)	.40					.35		
7. Cancer advocacy (5)							.25	
8. Peripherals (3)								.33

* Only proportions of .20 and greater are shown for ease of interpretation.

As in the earlier survey, the Core group was the group most nominated by those in other groups, with the Workforce and hospitals, State government – health, Public health, and Community based groups all nominating people in the core group. There is no obvious second group in terms of structural equivalence, as there was in 2001. Internal cohesion of the groups is now higher. The Core group is the most cohesive (with 43 per cent of nominations to people within this group), but the Community based, Peripherals, Cancer advocacy, and Public health groups are also reasonably cohesive.

Figure 3.2 shows this network block structure diagrammatically. In contrast with the earlier survey, the network now has only one central group; the other groups form a star shape around this core group. Some of the changes appear to relate to the longevity of the state government. In 2001 this government had been in power for less than two years and there were no distinct government groups generated by the blockmodelling. In 2004, the government had been in power for five years, and now two of the blocks are distinctively state government groups. Fewer medically qualified people and fewer men are included in 2004, which might reflect the impact of the movement of key medically qualified individuals out of this policy area and the impact of that on the snowballing in this case. It is not possible to make solid claims about whether this change is an artefact of the snowball sample, reflects changes occurring in the health sector, or is related to the different phase of the electoral cycle, with the government now in its second term.

Figure 3.2 Network of influence in health 2004

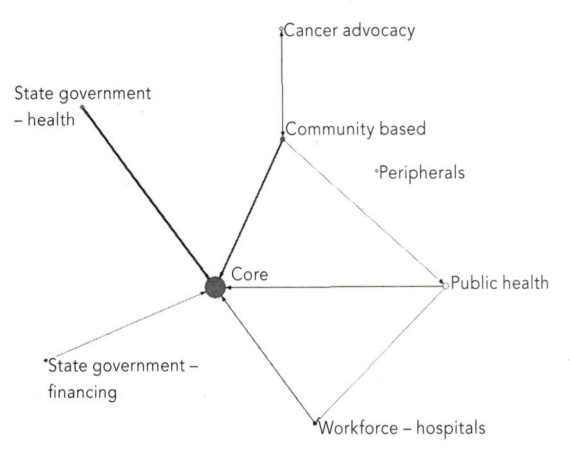

Influence • 103

Table 3.5 Centrality of individuals 2004*

	Centrality In-degree	Centrality Betweenness
Dean of Health Sciences, La Trobe University	32	18.0
CEO of VicHealth	19	33.5
Secretary, Department of Human Services	17	10.6
CEO of Bayside Health	13	1.7
Assoc Professor and Director of AIPC, La Trobe University	8	11.5
CEO of Austin Health	8	0.7
Chair of the VicHealth Board	7	22.9
Chair of Bio21	7	1.7
Director of Women's Health Victoria	6	11.4
Professor of Population Health, University of Melbourne	6	3.7
Director, Cancer Council of Victoria	6	3.0
Dean of Health Sciences, Deakin University	6	2.4
Director Breastscreen Vic	4	25.2

* Those included had an in-degree centrality score of 6 or more, plus the Director of Breastscreen, who had the second highest betweenness centrality of all 53 respondents.

The Dean of Health Sciences at La Trobe University again tops the list for in-degree centrality (see Table 3.5). The new Minister did not participate in this round and so does not appear on the list. Both of the medical deans had recently moved to new positions which were not specifically health related, so they both declined to nominate people this time. The CEOs of Vic Health and Bayside Health, and the Secretary of the Department of Human Services were again very central – and all three

104 • Connecting and Cooperating

of these are the same people as in 2001. Another hospital CEO has joined the most central list in 2004. The Director of the Cancer Council was central in both years.

The CEO of VicHealth has risen from fifth in 2001 to second in 2004, however, with the absence of the Minister and the two medical deans, this means that he has really just maintained his ranking. He also heads the betweenness centrality ranking, followed by the Director of Breastscreen and the Chair of the VicHealth Board. The Secretary of the Department is relatively low on this measure, as she was in 2001.

Table 3.6 lists the most important and difficult issues. These are a mix of the same issues as appeared in 2001 (workforce, demand in public hospitals, split responsibilities, the balance between acute care and disease prevention/health promotion), and new issues (chronic illness and obesity). As 2004 was a Federal election year, it is not surprising that split responsibilities between levels of government and across primary, hospital and aged care was on top of the list of concerns.

In relation to the linking of actors and issues, it remained true that the most central influential actors were interested in the most highly nominated issues. However, the picture was more mixed, with some very central people nominating public health-type issues, such as obesity, and moving the emphasis from acute care to more preventive approaches. In addition, and perhaps indicative of the length of time this government had been in place, was the correspondence of the most often mentioned issues with those working in state government, even when they were not very central to the network. This is an intriguing insight into the link between actors' issues of interest and their network locations, which points to the combination of influential people and their main areas of concern being a contributor to setting the policy agenda.

Table 3.6 Most important and difficult issues in 2004

Issue in health policy	Important issues	Difficult issues	Total
1. Split responsibilities (Commonwealth–state/territory, primary/acute/aged care)	13	2	15
2. Workforce structural changes	7	2	9
3. Need to shift balance from acute care to health promotion and disease prevention, under-investment in prevention	6	3	9
4. Increasing chronic illness	6	1	7
5. Demand for public hospital care	5	1	6
6. Overweight, obesity, nutrition	4	2	6
Structural determinants	4	0	4
Problems with Medicare, PHI, funding services	2	2	4
Upstream determinants of mental health and wellbeing	2	2	4
Lack of public funding for particular areas (dental, mental, community health)	2	2	4
Quality and safety of care	3	0	3
Information management and overcoming privacy issues	3	0	3
Lack of consumer perspectives, advocacy	1	2	3
Need for health services research rather than medical research	1	2	3
Alcohol and illicit drugs	1	2	3

Interpersonal violence	1	1	2
Cancer screening	2	0	2
Competing priorities of health and other areas in government	2	0	2
Pandemic infection control and bioterrorism	2	0	2
Aboriginal health	1	1	2
End of life decisions, rationing care	0	2	2
Abortion	1	0	1
Total	69	27	96

This use of a social capital framework as a means for understanding the public policy process demonstrates the utility of analysing network structure, the level of importance of individuals in network centrality and betweenness terms, and how they see themselves within this network. It shows that the issues that particular sub-groups of actors are interested in relate to their network connections, which in turn shape the policy agenda. Finally, it shows how actors and issues change over time. The embedded resources available to the most central actors in this network are considerable, and these actors can be observed using their connections to talk about and push forward their interests in certain issues with others who are close to them. This example of social capital arising from network connections demonstrates the impact that influential actors, both individuals and groups, with shared interests in issues, have on setting the policy agenda.

4 Innovation

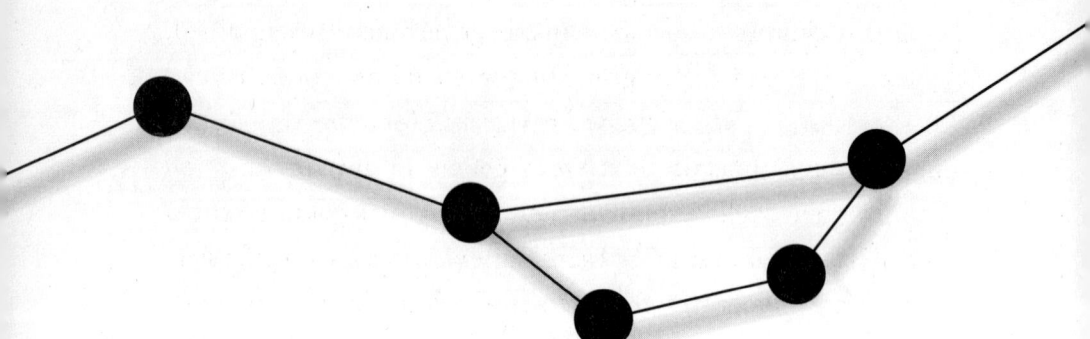

Social capital and its positive impact on economies have been linked to innovation and knowledge creation in a growing body of literature. Dense networks of firms, researchers and policy makers are seen as crucial in enabling innovation (Field 2003). A lot of relevant knowledge concerns not just *what* we need to know, but also the 'know-how' to apply it and the 'know-who' to apply it to (Maskell 2000). In other words, it is about people using their knowledge in particular settings of social relations.

Innovation has had scant attention paid to it as something that governments do, despite its potential for solving intractable problems and improving economic performance. Like influence in policy agenda setting, it is not usually seen through a framework of social capital, at least not in a governmental context. This is strange, since innovation is regarded as desirable by all, and in recent years many governments have begun to regard innovation as an important component of economic policy. Governments, even though they have a unique set of characteristics that generate a different set of constraints from those facing private firms, surely need to be innovative.

In this chapter, innovation inside government is examined. Like policy agenda setting, it rests on social networks. Unlike the previous chapter, where the networks of interest were based on influence connections between people in any organisation within a policy field, in this chapter, the networks of interest are those inside organisations. Using innovation as a specific way of thinking about policy achievements within governments, this chapter explores how social capital can help explain it.

Within all organisations, who people go to in order to get advice and find information is certainly shaped by the formal structure of that organisation. However, less formally structured networking also occurs, as people roam far and wide looking for information from wherever they can find it. They are rarely prohibited from seeking information beyond the silos of divisional boundaries. Neither are they usually limited to reaching only one level above or below their positions; they can skip levels to get the advice and information they need. However, informal communication will of course be shaped by organisational structures and status considerations.

Social capital in the case of innovation is seen to rest on the informal patterns of communication among actors. Being on the same committees and sharing portfolio responsibilities are also important in shaping who interacts with whom. Politicians and bureaucrats sit on different sides of governmental structures, and hierarchical level is bound to affect access to those in crucial positions. But informal networking also plays a significant role in organisational life. The previous chapter demonstrated that networks of influential actors have a set of embedded resources that can be used to wield informal power within a policy sector and to significantly shape the policy agenda. In this chapter the aim is to show how networks, and the resources they provide access to, can help innovation.

Innovation within governments

In the research literature on innovation inside government, there are accounts that stress the use of a systems approach and process improvement (Borins 2001) or system values (Swift 1993). Innovation successes occur, it is argued in this literature, when a whole system is geared towards innovative outcomes. Lundvall's (1992) book on national systems of innovation points to such properties. Conversely, some claim that innovation runs counter to existing structures and regard frustration with how things are currently done as a major reason for innovating. Many consider innovation to be an individual rather than collective property, or argue that innovative ideas come from everywhere (Walters 2001). Few attempts have been made to study innovation diffusion in relation to policy making. However, one study demonstrated that innovators use external and internal networks to get new items onto the policy agenda, and internal networks to get the required approvals (see Mintrom & Vergari 1998).

Examining innovation, and what it means to be an innovator, through the lens of social capital moves us past accounts that emphasise formal structures. A focus on communication between individuals provides rich information on the resources that actors can access through their network ties to others. Mapping who talks to whom, and where information is obtained and traded, opens up the possibility of a social capital explanation of innovation: as an outcome which is underpinned by informal links between individuals.

As is argued throughout this book, embedded resources are generated by social network ties between individuals. In innovation research there is a tradition of tracing how these forms of connectedness and exchange inside networks shape the way ideas are communicated, and the way new products and methods are distributed. Most of this research points to the critical role networks play in the diffusion of innovation, emphasising who influences whom (see Rogers 1995; Valente 1995). However, these innovation studies tend to focus not on the innovations themselves, but on how they are communicated across a defined population (see Coleman, Katz & Menzel 1957; Rogers & Beal 1958). While the emphasis on communication in these studies is to be applauded, the interest in this chapter is not on mapping innovations as they spread through groups of people, but on using a social capital framework as a means for identifying access to network resources and the relationship between that and who the innovators are.

The social capital framework developed in this book points to some actors having greater access to network resources than others. We have seen that in the previous chapter, where influential people were shown to be clustered into sub-groups that provide them with more or less power, and a greater or lesser ability to set the policy agenda. In this chapter, the puzzle is innovators and the kinds of network positions they hold, as a means for making claims about how social capital helps in understanding who the innovators are in a governmental context, and whether or not this is more important than the formal positions they hold. It adds to the argument that a social capital framework can be useful in analysing the public policy process.

The study used to test the social capital framework in this case is one on 11 local governments in Victoria. They participated in the project following a call for expressions of interest through the Victorian Local Governance Association (an umbrella industry association for local governments in Victoria).[1] Full details of this large study can be found in Considine, Lewis and Alexander (2009).

Senior bureaucrats (CEOs, directors, managers, and team leaders) and all politicians at each of the 11 participating local governments were surveyed using a questionnaire distributed at meetings of staff or through the internal mail system. In a small number of cases, the questionnaire was administered in person. The questionnaire collected information on respondents' social networks as well as asking a range of questions concerning how they framed innovation as a concept, and how different institutional, structural and personal traits influenced innovation in their municipality. Overall, 765 responses were received from the 947 people given questionnaires. This is an 80.8 per cent response rate.

In this chapter, only two crucial aspects of the study are described. One is the formal institutional position and the other is informal networks. Detailed analysis of the innovation dispositions of these 11 governments has been published elsewhere (see

Considine & Lewis 2005). A lengthy description of the level of external networking of people in these governments has also been described elsewhere (see Considine, Lewis & Alexander 2008). The focus here is on formal position and informal networks. Little needs to be said about structural position, beyond the assumed impact that location in the hierarchy has on innovator status, which is discussed later. Social network information was gathered to allow a detailed examination of informal communication. This is examined next, before assessing the importance of these networks to innovation.

Network structure

The central role that networks play in facilitating innovation and shaping innovation pathways at the organisational, sectoral and national level has been discussed at length in the literature on private sector innovation (see Conway 1995; Jones, Conway & Steward 1998; Love 1999). The importance of internal and cross-organisational relationships is also generally acknowledged within the public sector literature, particularly in the context of the diffusion of innovative ideas and practices.

Only a few studies have examined the structure of innovation networks within governments in any systematic fashion. These have shown that networks are a prime means of facilitating information exchange within organisations and governments. The innovative capacity of local governments has been linked to the presence of strong internal and external networks (Newman, Raine & Skelcher 2001). A number of studies have also noted the influence of network membership on the innovative capacity of public sector managers and elected officials, who use them as important forums for vetting new ideas and examining their fit with professional norms (Teske & Schneider 1994). Of course networks can also have a constraining influence, encouraging conformism to dominant perceptions of appropriate behaviour.

The social network data in this study was collected using a name generator, with respondents asked to nominate up to five people they went to most: first, when they wanted to get advice on a work-related issue; and second, when they wanted to get strategic information about something in their government.[2] Having collected the data for both networks in each government we mapped the network structures to provide a visualisation of the global and local patterns of communication in different governments.

Advice network maps are shown in Figures 4.1 and 4.2, and strategic information networks in Figures 4.3 and 4.4. The governments have been given pseudonyms. The mapping option used here places those with the most network ties in the middle and those with fewer ties around the periphery. These are ego network maps for the mayors and CEOs in these governments. That is, they are the networks that immediately surround the mayors and CEOs, made up of all actors with a direct tie (either in or out or reciprocal) to both of these actors.

Figure 4.1 shows that the Mayor and CEO of Parkside are integrated and have substantially overlapping networks for advice. There is a fairly clear star shape around the CEO, comprised mostly of bureaucrats, with some external people. The

Figure 4.1 Parkside advice network around the CEO and Mayor

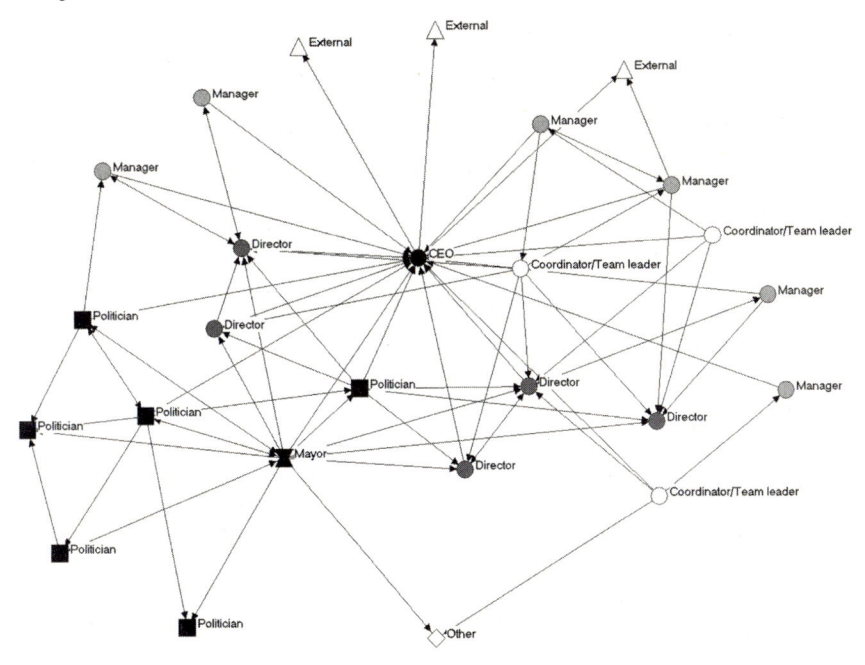

Figure 4.2 Oberon advice network around the CEO and Mayor

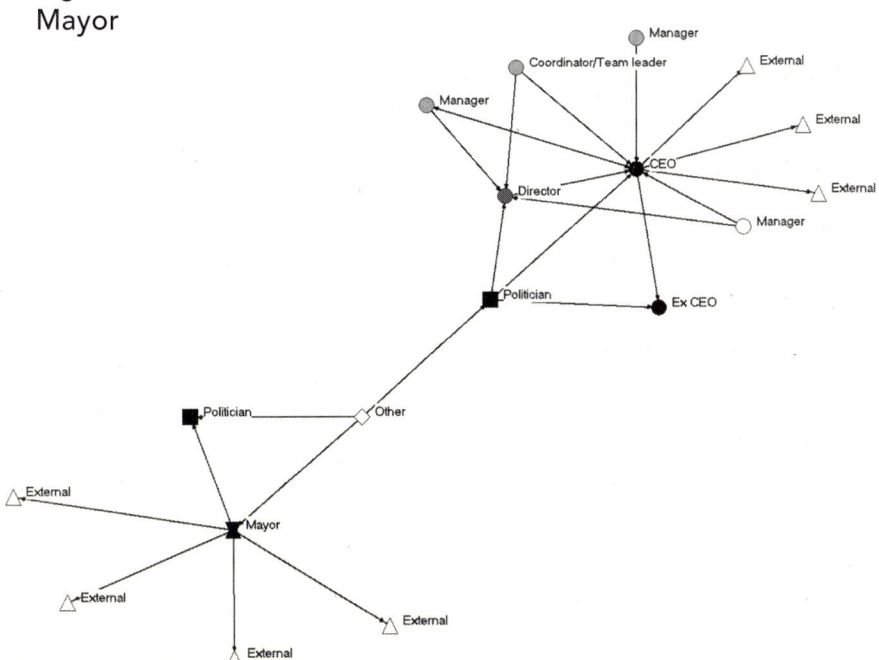

Figure 4.3 Parkside strategic information network around the CEO and Mayor

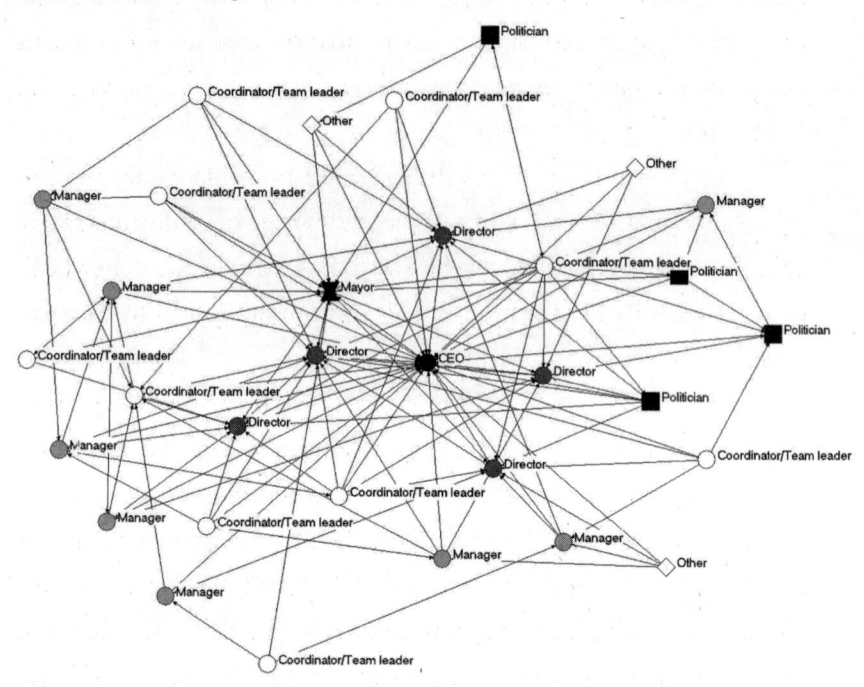

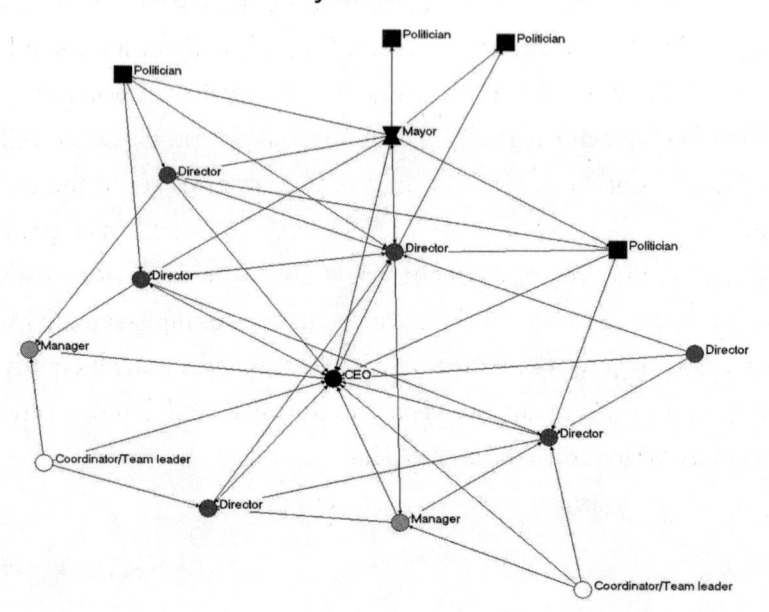

Figure 4.4 Wallerstrum strategic information network around the CEO and Mayor

politicians are concentrated on the lower left-hand side of the map and clustered around the Mayor. There are direct ties between the Mayor and three other politicians and the CEO in this government. There are also several ties between bureaucrats and politicians.

In contrast, Figure 4.2 is the extreme example where the political arm is almost entirely separated from the administrative arm. The Mayor of Oberon has an advice tie to one other politician and one other person in this government, and to four external people.

Figures 4.3 and 4.4 present the strategic information ego networks for the mayors and CEOs at Parkside and Wallerstrum. The combined CEO and Mayor strategic information ego network at Parkside (see Figure 4.3) is the most elaborate of the 11 governments. Indeed, the Parkside CEO and Mayor each individually have the largest ego networks of all their bureaucratic and political colleagues respectively. In total, there are 27 actors in the CEO's network, including the Mayor and three other politicians, four of the five directors, eight managers, and 11 others. The Mayor's network is smaller, with 15 actors, including the CEO and all five directors, and two other politicians.

There is a reciprocal tie linking the Mayor and CEO, as well as a large number of ties linking the senior members of the bureaucracy to the politicians. Overall there are 17 ties linking the politicians and senior bureaucrats (CEO and directors), with the majority of these (14) being politicians seeking strategic information from bureaucrats. This again suggests quite a closely integrated relationship between the political and bureaucratic branches of government at Parkside.

In contrast, Figure 4.4 shows the smallest combined CEO and Mayor strategic information ego network, with 16 actors. Here, the CEO's network contains just 12 actors, including the Mayor, one other politician, six directors, two managers and two coordinators/team leaders. The Mayor's network contains eight actors – the CEO, three directors and all four of the other politicians. There is a small degree of overlap between the two networks, with one politician and three directors appearing in both. In marked contrast to Parkside, there are no mid-level bureaucrats in the Mayor's ego network at Wallerstrum, and just four in the CEO's network. This configuration suggests that in this government, the strategic information network is heavily influenced by hierarchy. There is also a clear distinction between the political and administrative sides of government at Wallerstrum, with the politicians concentrated around the Mayor at the top of Figure 4.4.

Centrality

These network maps provide a useful visualisation of social structure. Social network measures for individual actors provide more precision about network effects, and address the question of what impact these informal networks have on innovation. A multivariate approach is required to analyse the relative contribution networks make compared with the effects of the formal hierarchical positions and different roles of these actors.

To take this multivariate step, individual network scores for advice and strategic information are required. The in-degree centrality of each of the respondents was calculated, to provide a measure of the prominence of each of these actors in network terms. The most important or prestigious actors are usually those with large in-degrees (Wasserman & Faust 1994). In this example, in-degree means the extent to which other actors go to a particular person in search of advice or strategic information.

Table 4.1 shows mean in-degree centrality scores grouped by positions for four of the 11 governments. These four were selected to participate in the more detailed second stage of the research, and were chosen because of their diversity in terms of socioeconomic status (SES) of the citizens, political orientation of the governments, whether they were close to Melbourne's city centre or further out, their dominant innovation norms and views of governance, and their different levels of external engagement and network structures. They can be characterised as:

- Kilbourne – fringe metro, lower and middle SES, swing seats
- Melville – middle metro, upper middle SES, solid conservative
- Millside – inner metro, old working class and gentrified, solid Labor
- Parkside – inner metro, gentrified, Labor/Green.

The scores in Table 4.1 are normalised (and hence do not refer simply to the number of times an individual was mentioned).[3]

The results show that CEOs are the most central actors for advice, followed by directors and then managers, in all four governments (see Table 4.1). In other words, hierarchy rules for advice-seeking behaviour, with ties being directed up the ladder. Politicians are only as central as the coordinators/team leaders, and others. There are some variations across governments in relation to this overall trend, but the pattern holds. Politicians were never more central than bureaucrats: advice is sought more often from the bureaucrats than from them.

Table 4.1 Network centrality by position (mean in-degree centrality)

	Mayor	Politician	CEO	Director	Manager	Coordinator/ Team leader	Other
Advice							
Kilbourne	1.32	1.10	14.47	12.63	6.17	0.70	1.03
Melville	2.33	1.55	25.58	16.86	4.51	1.40	0.93
Millside	1.82	0.00	21.82	13.45	4.00	2.25	2.31
Parkside	3.49	2.62	18.60	11.63	3.94	1.46	1.42
Strategic information							
Kilbourne	5.26	2.41	11.84	20.26	9.95	0.93	0.94
Melville	4.76	2.38	38.10	32.14	6.85	1.43	0.95
Millside	10.91	3.64	58.18	42.91	12.55	2.99	4.96
Parkside	12.79	2.03	31.40	19.53	5.55	1.31	1.03

Centrality scores for strategic information indicate that CEOs and directors are again the most central, although the directors are more central than the CEO at Kilbourne. Managers follow in three of the four governments. The Mayors at Millside and Parkside are, respectively, very close to the managers, or ahead of them, in terms of centrality. For all four governments, politicians – and especially Mayors – are relatively more central for strategic information than for advice networks. It seems that politicians have a stronger network role to play as sources of strategic information than as sources of advice.

Key innovators

Interviews were conducted with 104 respondents from across the four governments (approximately 26 in each) in the second stage of the study, to gain a more detailed understanding of the nature of innovation at each location. During this round of interviews, respondents were asked to identify important innovations in their municipality, to detail who was involved in each case, and to nominate the key innovators in their municipality.[4] No limitations were placed on the number of 'key innovator' nominations that could be made, and the latter could include politicians, bureaucrats, or people outside the government.[5]

To enable the identification of the innovators at each municipality and to test their innovator status against a range of variables, a key innovator score based on these nominations was used. Politicians and bureaucrats at each municipality who had completed the initial survey were assigned a score reflecting the percentage of total key innovator nominations they received from the interview respondents in their municipality, with those not nominated assigned a score of zero. As the results in Table 4.2 indicate, scores on this scale ranged from 0 to a high of 16.8 at Kilbourne, 13.4 at Millside, 12.4 at Parkside and 10.3 at Melville. The standard deviation figures suggest that variation on the scale was highest at Millside (3.5) and lowest at Parkside (2.2).

Table 4.2 Key innovator scores (percentage)

	Kilbourne	Melville	Millside	Parkside	Total
N	78	44	57	89	268
Mean	1.3	2.3	1.8	1.1	1.5
Std deviation	2.9	3.0	3.5	2.2	2.8
Minimum	0	0	0	0	0
Maximum	16.8	10.3	13.4	12.4	16.8

The next question is how important networks, roles and positions are in determining innovator status. Is it the authority that comes from the role of politician or bureaucrat, or the level in the hierarchy, or the connections based on communication and information exchange, that best explains who is, and who is not, regarded as an innovator? A multivariate approach was used to examine the relative effects of formal (hierarchical) and informal (network) structures, in order to make claims about the importance of social capital for innovation. To examine what contributes to innovator status, multiple regression was used, with the key innovator score as the dependent variable. The two network centrality variables were highly correlated (not surprisingly).

These descriptions of who the innovators are in terms of formal roles and network positions point to a fundamental tension. On one hand there are important differences in the way each municipality is structured in network terms, with vastly different patterns of connections around the two key actors (the Mayor and the CEO). On the other hand, it seems that hierarchical position is an important influence on patterns of connectedness – perhaps countering or moderating the effect of less formal networks. It is also clear that who is most crucial varies by network type, and that politicians and bureaucrats have varying importance depending on whether the network involves advice or information.

The important relationship between structural position and innovator status has also been noted: successful innovators tend to reside further up the hierarchy, where they are able to profit from the strategic benefits that seniority confers. To measure the relative impact of structural position on innovator status a set of dichotomous variables for position was included in the regressions. The largest group of respondents in the study was coordinators/team leaders (44 per cent of the total). This group is used as the reference category for the regression analysis, enabling measurement of the relative effect of being positioned at the level of Mayor, politician, CEO, director, manager, or other on innovator status.

Since the two network measures were highly correlated, two separate regressions were run, with advice centrality included as an independent variable in one, and strategic information centrality included in the other. Networks and positions both turned out to be important predictors of innovator status. The results, showing the regression results using forced entry of the same set of variables into each of the regression equations, are provided in Tables 4.3 and 4.4.

Strategic information network centrality is a significant predictor of recognition as an innovator in two of the four governments, and overall (see Table 4.3). If you are seen to be an innovator, you will also be someone a lot of people come to for strategic information. Being a politician is a predictor in three of the four governments, as well as overall. The CEO role was significant in two of the four governments as well as overall. This analysis suggests that both networks and positions are important in shaping perceived innovator status, with networks the only important factor in predicting who is seen as an innovator in one government, and position the only important factor in two other governments. Both network and position are significant in the fourth government, and in the total sample.

Table 4.3 Innovators with strategic information networks and position

	Kilbourne	Melville	Millside	Parkside	All
N	88	53	62	93	296
Adjusted R-Squared	.30	.39	.62	.60	.39
Strategic information network centrality	.63			.41	.43
Position (ref: Coordinator/Team Leader)					
Mayor				.47	.12
Politician		.44	.56	.47	.33
CEO			.27	.31	.14
Director			.35		
Manager					.13
Other					

Standardised regression coefficients statistically significant at p = 0.05.
Dependent variable = percentage of 'Key innovator' nominations per government.
Regressions conducted using the enter method.

The regression analysis that included strategic information networks indicates that, among the different types of position within these governments, being a politician is the strongest predictor of innovator status, although CEOs are also important innovators (see Table 4.3). Being a director was an important predictor of innovator status at Millside. These regressions indicate that both formal position and informal network relationships are important, and while there must be some overlap between these, given that it is impossible to separate interpersonal connections from hierarchical positions, they are not exactly the same.

Table 4.4 Innovators with advice networks and position

	Kilbourne	Melville	Millside	Parkside	All
N	88	53	62	93	296
Adjusted R-Squared	.16	.37	.63	.59	.34
Advice network centrality					.21
Position (ref: Coordinator/ Team Leader)					
Mayor			.48		.16
Politician		.45	.57	.47	.34
CEO			.25	.40	.22
Director			.34		.24
Manager	.31		.20		.21
Other					

Standardised regression coefficients statistically significant at p = 0.05.
Dependent variable = percentage of 'Key innovator' nominations per government.
Regressions conducted using the enter method.

The results were different for advice networks. Institutional position is more important in predicting innovator status than advice network centrality (see Table 4.4). Position is a significant predictor of innovator status in all four governments while advice network centrality was not significant in any of the four, although it was significant in the total sample. Again, being a politician was the strongest predictor of innovator status in all governments except Kilbourne. Interestingly, in two governments, as well as overall, being a manager was associated with being an innovator.

These analyses show that networks are important, and explain more than can be discovered by a focus on position alone. But different types of networks are not equally important. Advice networks are weakly related to being an innovator; strategic information networks appear more crucial. If you are seen as the person to go to for strategic information, you are also very likely to be seen as an innovator. The findings from Mintrom and Vergari's (1998) study indicate that different networks are important for different phases of innovation. It seems that strategic information centrality might be more important for innovator recognition because these actors are doing the visible, internal work of getting innovations approved and in place. Scanning for ideas outside the organisation through advice networks might well lead to initiation of innovation, but this is more intangible and diffuse.

With strategic information centrality being more important than position in the hierarchy in terms of status as an innovator, and the position of politician being a significant predictor of innovator status, and this being more important than advice network centrality, it seems that certain types of networks are more important than role or hierarchical position in explaining innovation. Innovators inhabit a particular social and institutional location, defined in part by their formal role and position, but more by their connections in informal networks, which generates their access to embedded resources and hence their social capital. They are in locations that have scope for movement, despite their structural constraints. In other words, they have a large potential for accessing the resources that accompany both their formal positions and their informal networks.

This chapter examined how structural positions and informal networks contribute to an explanation of innovation inside government. The results clearly show that what position you hold, and who you communicate with, are significant in shaping whether or not you are regarded as an innovator. However, network relationships of certain types are the most important predictors of innovator status. Although network centrality is not completely independent from hierarchical seniority, and it is not possible to assess the separate contribution of these two variables, our findings fit with the view that innovators are those who are adept at working through relationships outside formal structures in order to get things done inside governments. In the terms of this book, they are actors who have substantial social capital, and therefore have access to resources that are helpful in changing public policy.

5 Partnerships

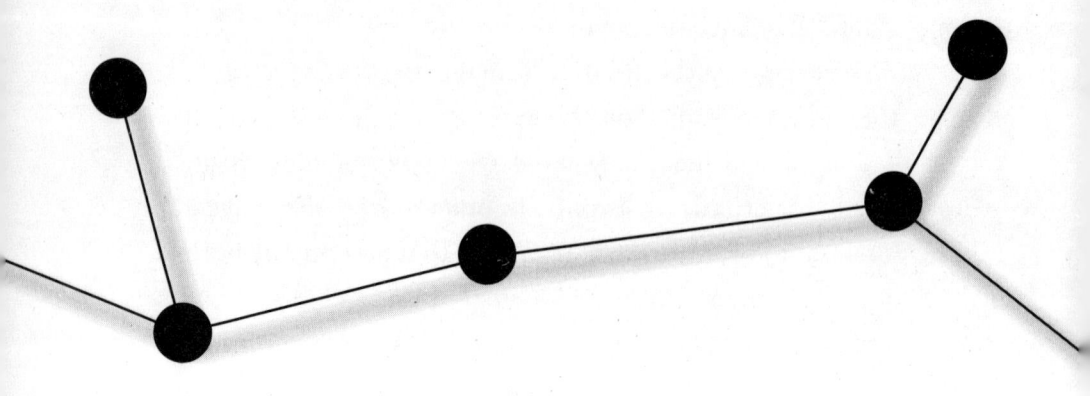

The term 'partnerships' is the catch phrase for an enormous variety of arrangements, from public–private partnerships, which are essentially contracts between private for-profit organisations and governments (or public organisations), to memoranda of understanding that involve a large number of organisations across sectors and levels of government. This first chapter of two on public policy as an intervention that aims to increase social capital examines partnerships where the policy intention is to build relationships between organisations. 'Partnerships', in this chapter, refers to attempts to join up actors – both individuals and organisations – at the local level.

Two different types of partnership are examined. These can be broadly categorised as those that focus on service coordination (partnerships between service providers with consumer/community input) and those that are about community building (government–community partnerships). The specific examples used both come from Victoria. The first (service coordination) are Primary Care Partnerships (PCPs), mandated and funded by the Department of Human Services, and the second (community building) are a range of partnerships funded by the Department of Planning and Community Development. These include partnerships funded by the Community Building Initiative, Community Renewal, Regional Sports Assemblies, and Transport Connections, as well as an Aboriginal Council of Australian Governments partnership, and a partnership between a developer and a local government.

While the first type of partnership is squarely addressing service coordination problems in primary healthcare, the second is about building communities to address disadvantage of various kinds. Both are policies that attempt to build social capital, but in different ways. The health partnerships aim to encourage links between individuals in different service provider organisations, in order to overcome fragmented service delivery at the local level. The emphasis is on organisations building relationships to increase their understanding of what other organisations operating in the same locality do; it is hoped that this will result in improved services for clients. This clearly serves an instrumental purpose, but it has social capital aspects in its focus on relationship building. It is less obviously about social capital than the community development partnership, but it fits the social capital framework used in this book as an intervention to generate connections and access to resources through these.

Government funding provided the impetus for both these types of partnership, and they are, to varying degrees, centrally driven, with the rules of engagement stipulated. Though their central aims, as well as who was to be involved and what their scope of concern was to be, were mandated by the relevant departments in both groups, this was more the case for the PCPs than for the community development partnerships.

These partnerships can be thought of as a particular form of network governance: a form of governing that is based on a mode of organisation that is cooperative, rather than competitive (as in markets) or hierarchical (as in bureaucracies) (Powell 1990). Network governance is described in more detail later in the next section. This raises questions about what kind of network structure is required for building social capital, and what can be done to ascertain whether these partnerships have that structure. A set of network characteristics is proposed, and the partnerships are examined against them. Outcomes are important for these partnerships, as they are funded to achieve certain things.

Partnerships have conceptual appeal in addressing contemporary governance challenges, and they represent a local manifestation of network governance in practice (Lewis 2005a). This chapter seeks to answer questions about whether they build social capital through strengthening inter-organisational relationships. The outcomes of the health partnerships should accrue to the organisations involved and their clients. The outcomes for the community partnerships are more diffuse in that they should accrue to the local community in general. However, there should also be outcomes for the organisations involved: it is believed that there are benefits to be gained from being linked to other organisations in one's local area, and to government.

Using social capital as a framework to examine these partnerships means that there is a need to be very explicit about what a 'good' network structure for these partnerships consists of, and to pay attention to how they can be evaluated to assess whether they are working or not (building social capital or not), and generating the desired outcomes.

'Partnerships' is a term that covers a multitude of governance arrangements. Here it is taken to mean a set of arrangements between organisations at the local level, involving different levels of government and different sectors, and reflects a mode of governing that rests on cooperation. Partnerships are formal arrangements introduced by a central authority to support joint action to achieve a particular objective. The fundamentals of network governance are examined next.

Network governance

An often-used three-way classification of modes of governance is hierarchies, markets and networks. These three types are conceptually distinct, reflecting coordination mechanisms that rest on authority (hierarchies), competition (markets) and collaboration (networks).

During the 1980s, the imperatives for the public sector to cut costs and maximise outputs grew. Public organisations were expected to emulate businesses, and focus on competition, contracts and consumer choice. This peaked in the early 1990s in the UK, and was followed by changes which aimed to address the challenges of coordinating actors from the many and varied sectors now involved in governing. The state, incorporating many actors, requires coordination to steer society through the control of critical resources, and it needs to achieve this by co-ordinating interests, rather than by using legal powers (Rhodes 1997; Pierre & Peters 2000). The metaphor of the network began to be used to describe the large number of diverse agencies involved in governing, making policy and delivering public services, in the context of both greater fragmentation and greater congestion. Networks, where the mode of coordination is based on relationships, became an alternative to hierarchies, where the mode of coordination is command, and markets, where it is price (Thompson et al. 1991; Considine & Lewis 1999; 2003).

Network governance is both a description of, and a proposed solution to, the need for coordination. Competition was replaced by 'joined-up-government' or 'whole-of-government' approaches to these new governing challenges. Where government cannot impose policy but must negotiate with a range of organisations that have a significant amount of autonomy, governance is now focused on steering networks (Rhodes 2000; Powell & Exworthy 2002). Networks are a form of governance that is seen as more suitable today, as many contemporary problems are complex and cannot be divided up into pieces and treated as independent.

How does this link to partnerships? There is now a substantial literature describing partnerships that involve coalitions of organisations addressing issues that require a diversity of expertise and resources (see Skelcher et al. 1996; Mandell 2001; Agranoff 2007). They represent efforts to institutionalise the positive effects of networking (such as increasing diversity by involving a greater range of actors) through requiring more formal connections between organisations (O'Toole 1997). Partnerships undertake activities that go beyond what could be achieved by individual organisations alone. As partnerships are based on the formation and maintenance of relationships, they require a kind of management that relies on network facilitation (O'Toole 1997; Mandell 2001; Sullivan & Skelcher 2002; Keast et al. 2004). A partnership facilitator, or 'broker', undertakes tasks related to managing behaviours: activating the right people, 'blending' participants with different goals and norms, and establishing operating rules for them to deal with operational complexity, for example (Agranoff & McGuire 2001).

The partnerships of interest in this chapter are government initiated and funded, but involve different tiers of government and public, private for-profit and private not-for-profit agencies. They are centrally steered and monitored, and they have government-funded network coordinators. They are geographically defined and leadership is undertaken by formal agencies rather than by mobilised communities. It needs to be recognised that these are a particular type of network: a 'managed network' (Lewis 2005a). This shapes the kind of network that will emerge and the type of social capital likely to be generated.

Partnerships that are externally mandated, and funded at least partially by government, such as those under discussion in this chapter, combine network principles with hierarchy and market principles. The term 'partnership' tends to generate an expectation from those involved in them of flatter structures than traditional hierarchies, and of more trust and egalitarianism. This view casts them as superior in terms of democracy, inclusiveness and equality. However, power differentials do not disappear when actors become part of a partnership. Equally, while the network metaphor might signal a more egalitarian, democratic and inclusive form of governance, this is not necessarily what transpires in all types of partnership (Lewis 2004) or in all forms of network governance (Sorenson & Torfing 2007; Klijn & Skelcher 2007). Partnerships can be more interested in engaging recognised groups and delivering efficiency than in increasing representation and equity. They do not automatically improve networks and increase social capital.

The rise of partnerships as a means of addressing a range of policy problems has been followed by the recognition that evaluating them is by no means simple (Milward & Provan 1998). Nonetheless, policy makers and practitioners need evaluation information to assess whether or not a partnership is performing well as a governing entity, whether or not better decision making than would have been possible through the actions of single organisations has resulted, and whether or not desired outcomes have been achieved (Provan & Milward 2001; Agranoff & McGuire 2001; Benington 2001; Sullivan & Skelcher 2002). Examining outcomes is particularly challenging because partnership work is focused on complex issues, where outcomes take time. In the short term, information about a partnership's performance in terms of the relationships that have been built and the decisions that have been made needs to be used to make judgments about effectiveness.

A set of characteristics of partnerships, using network concepts, is needed to examine whether or not relationships are being built, and thus whether or not social capital is also being built. These are hypothesised to be:

1. All core partners should be central and connected
2. Network brokers should be in very central positions
3. The funding agency should not be the most central actor
4. Over time, as people enter and exit, brokers and the core agencies should remain central
5. Redundancy should be high so that removing a small number of actors would not fragment the network
6. The connections with others should be positively valued by the actors in the network, and used to achieve things that could not be achieved alone
7. The partnerships should be sustainable over the longer term either with continuing funding or alternative ongoing brokerage and steering arrangements.

In the late 1990s in Victoria, following almost a decade of managerialism and privatisation, and the amalgamation of local governments, primary healthcare was facing further contracting arrangements and more rationalisation of services (Department of Human Services [DHS] 1998). The newly elected Bracks (Labor) Government set a new direction, focused on coordination through partnerships (DHS 2000). Primary Care Partnerships were established as part of this change in direction. In 2002 the Department for Victorian Communities was created and a range of community development partnerships aimed at reducing disadvantage were subsequently established (Department of Planning and Community Development 2007).

Primary Care Partnerships

An important challenge in delivering health and related services is the need to coordinate many separate organisations, varying widely in size and scope of service provision. This is particularly true in Australia, with its complicated and confusing funding and service provision responsibilities. Australian states and territories retain the major responsibility for health service provision. The Commonwealth's role has tended to be limited to funding hospitals, medical services and pharmaceuticals, while the states and territories deliver services either directly or indirectly. Municipal governments also provide healthcare and private for-profit and not-for-profit organisations are heavily involved in health service provision.

Primary Care Partnerships (PCPs) are aimed at improving service coordination and so, ultimately, improving health (see the stated aims below). So, do they build social capital? Just as importantly, how can an assessment be made of whether or not these partnerships build social capital? I answer this by applying the list of ideal (network) characteristics of partnerships. But before that, the aims, funding arrangements and partners involved are briefly described.

PCPs were introduced in 2001. The aim, as noted above, was to improve the health and wellbeing of a catchment's population by better coordination of planning and service delivery (DHS 2000). A second aim was to improve the experience of and outcomes for recipients, and reduce the preventable use of hospital, medical and residential services. The PCP strategy essentially retained the purchaser–provider split between DHS and service providers, and overlaid it with a collaborative approach to improving service delivery and outcomes.

The DHS provided one-off establishment funding to each PCP on signing a partnership agreement. This, plus other PCP funding, was used to develop community health plans, and to employ network coordinators (brokers) as well as staff in service coordination and health promotion roles. From 2000–01 to 2003–04, funding was allocated to PCPs for coordination and planning activities, information and communications technology infrastructure, and other projects. The initial four-year funding agreement was extended for two years, with reduced funding for service coordination and health promotion; in 2006, PCPs were granted recurrent funding.

Each PCP is required to include five core agencies – community health services (local centres employing a range of health professionals, funded mainly by state government); local governments; district nursing services; Divisions of General Practice (voluntary associations of GPs located in the same geographically defined area); and aged care assessment services (generally run by hospital out-patient services). Each PCP must also have a minimum of two other partner agencies, with those included chosen by the PCP on the basis of local priorities. There are 31 of them across the state. The DHS central office role is one of policy direction and advice, and DHS regional offices are responsible for their local PCPs' monitoring and accountability. PCPs usually cover two or three local government areas, although one has just a single local government partner.

Two PCPs (one city and one rural) were studied during 2001–05. Details of this can be found in Lewis (2005a; 2005b) and Lewis, Baeza and Alexander (2008).[1] One of them is in inner Melbourne (Westbay) and the other is in a rural area about 200 kilometres from the Melbourne metropolitan area (Campaspe). In socioeconomic terms, the inner metropolitan partnership covers a relatively poor area. The rural partnership is not wealthy compared with other parts of the state, but is wealthier, has an older age profile, and is less culturally diverse than the inner metropolitan partnership.

Steering committee members from each of these partnerships were interviewed in three successive years. These members included PCP project staff, partner agency staff involved in the PCP, and staff from the regional office of the DHS (who generally have a representative on the PCPs in their geographical area). Some people were interviewed in each of the three years, and others only once or twice, as staff moved on to new jobs in organisations outside the partnerships.[2] In the second year, six staff from the central office of DHS (all with some responsibility for PCPs) were interviewed, in relation to the policy direction of PCPs and the governing role of DHS. Over the three years of the study, where the same people were still involved they were reinterviewed, and where they had been replaced the new incumbent was interviewed.

The interview schedule itself was divided into a semi-structured component, allowing for open-ended responses to questions about relationships between organisations, and the achievements of PCPs to date, and a structured component, which was used to generate the network data. This involved asking respondents who they were in communication with in order to do their work, and who they went to for strategic information.[3] These two questions were used to distinguish between day-to-day communication about work issues, and a more deliberate form of information-seeking behaviour. No limitations were placed on the number of names that could be listed.[4] The open-ended questions added to the analysis of network structure by illustrating contextual factors and providing a more evaluative examination of relationships than could be gained from simply examining the network structures.

The information on network ties forms the basis of the network maps and analysis. More people were mentioned than appear in these diagrams (as interviewees were free to nominate whoever they chose), but only interviewees are included here. That is, a larger number of people were mentioned in both PCPs, but those named but not surveyed did not have the chance to nominate people in return. Network analysis relies on people being able to both be nominated and to nominate others in return, so only those interviewed are included in the analysis.

A first step towards this PCP's goals is engaging more people and building stronger relationships. As in earlier chapters, network maps and network measures are used to highlight the overall concentration and dispersion of the network, and the importance of particular individuals and agencies. The set of ideal characteristics for partnerships outlined above guides this analysis. Narrative descriptions of partnerships provide insights on agency – in this case, whether or not those involved are using and valuing the partnerships.

Network structures

Figure 5.1 is a map of the ties between actors in Campaspe PCP. The partnership staff are squares and all others are circles. Node size relates to the number of ties sent and received, and so is a measure of the amount of traffic to and from each person within this partnership. This gives an overall picture of network structure, but measures such as in-degree centrality (based on the number of ties directed towards an individual) are needed to find out the importance of particular actors. In these partnerships, an actor with a large centrality score is one who many other actors nominated as a contact in order to do their work and get strategic information. This measure is dependent upon network size, so a normalised figure was used which makes results comparable across these two networks, which are of different sizes.

Table 5.1 lists the top five ranked actors on the in-degree centrality measure for the work and strategic information networks at Campaspe and Westbay, and for each of the three years of the study. There are some underlying differences in the types of actors involved in each of the strategic information networks, which relate to the composition of the steering committees of the two partnerships. At Westbay, many more of the actors are from local government because there are three local governments represented on the steering committee. The strategic information network centrality results for Year 1 (top right-hand corner of Table 5.1), shows that at Campaspe, the PCP Manager (broker) and two PCP staff members were most central in the network, with an officer from the DHS Regional Office (208) and two local government representatives also relatively prominent. For Westbay, while the PCP Manager (broker) is likewise the most central actor, the next most prominent actor is the PCP Chair, followed by a DHS regional official, with the two PCP staff members in fourth and fifth positions. Centrality measures for the work network indicate that the very top positions tend to be occupied by the same actors as in the strategic information network, with some small changes in the top five.

Table 5.1 Primary Care Partnership top 5 actors ranked by centrality

		Work		Strategic information	
		Campaspe	Westbay	Campaspe	Westbay
Year 1		PCP CEO 201	PCP Manager 1	PCP CEO 201	PCP Manager 1
		PCP Staff 202	PCP Chair 3	PCP Staff 202	PCP Chair 3
		PCP Staff 203	PCP Staff 6	PCP Staff 203	DHS Region 16
		DHS Region 208	Comm Health A 13	DHS Region 208	PCP Staff 6
		Local Govt A 205	PCP Staff 9	Local Govt A 205	PCP Staff 9
		Hospital B 213		Local Govt A 216	
		PCP Chair 217			
Year 2		PCP Staff 203	PCP Manager 1	PCP Staff 203	PCP Manager 1
		PCP Staff 202	PCP Staff 6	PCP Staff 202	PCP Chair 46
		DHS Region 208	DHS Region 5	DHS Region 208	PCP Staff 6
		Local Govt A 205	PCP Chair 46	PCP Chair 217	Comm Health A13
		PCP Chair 217	Comm Health A 13	Local Govt A 205	Division of GP 12
				Hospital A 210	Other 136
				Hospital B 212	DHS Region 5
					DHS Region 92
Year 3		PCP Staff 202	PCP Manager 1	PCP Staff 202	PCP Manager 1
		Comm Health 203	PCP Chair 46	PCP Staff 408	PCP Chair 46
		PCP Staff 408	Comm Health A13	Local Govt A 205	Comm Health A 13
		Local Govt A 205	Other 136	Comm Health 203	PCP Staff 509
		Hospital A 342	PCP Staff 509		

Note: More than five are included where there are tied rankings

In addition to examining the centrality of individuals, it is also useful to analyse the centrality of the organisations in the partnership. Table 5.2 lists the percentage of in-degree ties directed towards organisational groups within the work networks. These are calculated by grouping the individual actors by organisational affiliation, aggregating the number of ties directed towards each group, and then expressing this figure as a percentage of total network ties. Only the work networks are presented and discussed here, but the results for the strategic information networks were similar.

Table 5.2 Percentage of ties to organisations for work networks

	Year 1	Year 2	Year 3
Campaspe			
PCP Staff	38.5	30.6	32.2
PCP Chair	7.7	6.1	7.8
Hospitals	10.3	17.1	20.0
Community Health	7.7	2.7	17.8
Local government	16.7	12.6	16.7
DHS region	16.7	18.9	3.3
Division of GP	1.3	1.8	0.0
Other	1.3	9.9	2.2
Westbay			
PCP Staff	36	38.8	44.4
PCP Chair	13.3	10.2	19.4
Hospitals	1.3	8.2	0.0
Community Health	10.7	8.2	11.1
Local government	22.7	8.2	13.9
DHS region	9.3	12.2	0.0
Division of GP	4.0	0.0	2.8
Other	2.7	14.3	8.3

The first column in Table 5.2 shows that for both of these partnerships, the largest proportion of ties in Year 1 were to partnership staff (broker agency). This was followed by local government, which came a clear second in Westbay, and tied for second with the DHS regional staff in Campaspe. For Westbay the partnership chair was the next most important, while for Campaspe it was hospital staff. DHS central office does not feature highly on these measures for either individuals or the organisation.

Network dynamics

The composition and structure of these networks shift from year to year as actors enter and leave, and personal and institutional relationships change. Figures 5.1, 5.2 and 5.3 show this dynamism in the work network at Campaspe. Figure 5.1 shows a fairly open structure, with 78 ties linking the 18 actors in the network. The PCP Manager (201) and two PCP staff, along with a bureaucrat from the DHS regional office (208), clearly dominate. One individual from a local hospital, a local government representative, another DHS officer (214) and the PCP Chair were also prominent.

Figure 5.2 shows a much more connected structure in the second year. There are now 111 ties linking the actors in the network. There has been significant turnover, with seven of the 20 network members from the previous year having changed. However, the two PCP staff remain central players in the network, as does one of the original members from the DHS

Figure 5.1 Campaspe work network, year 1

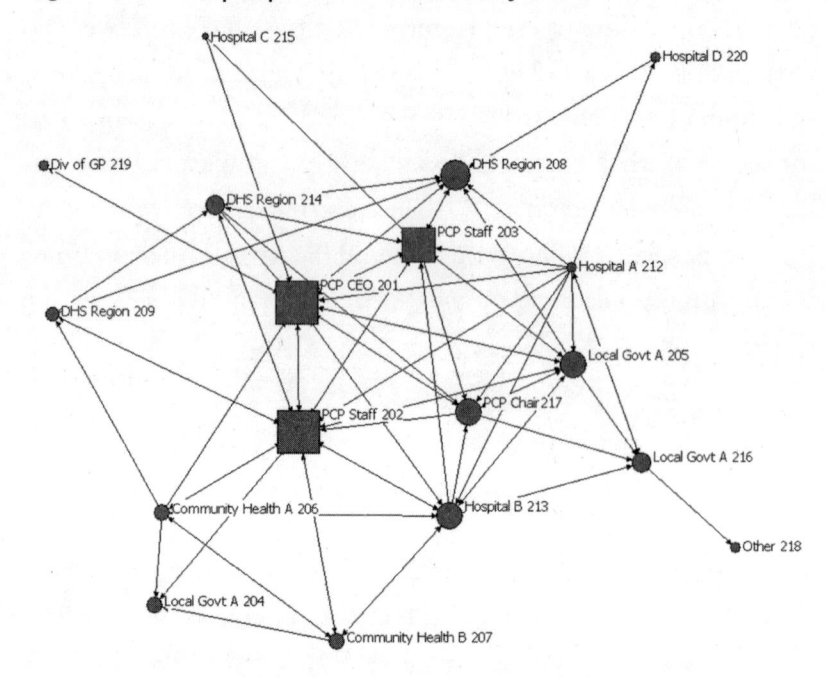

Figure 5.2 Campaspe work network, year 2

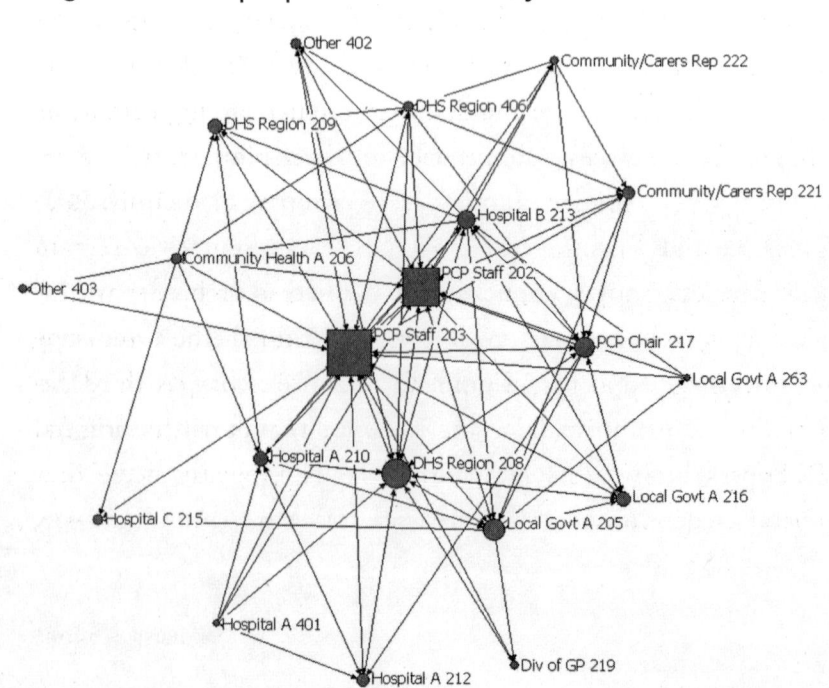

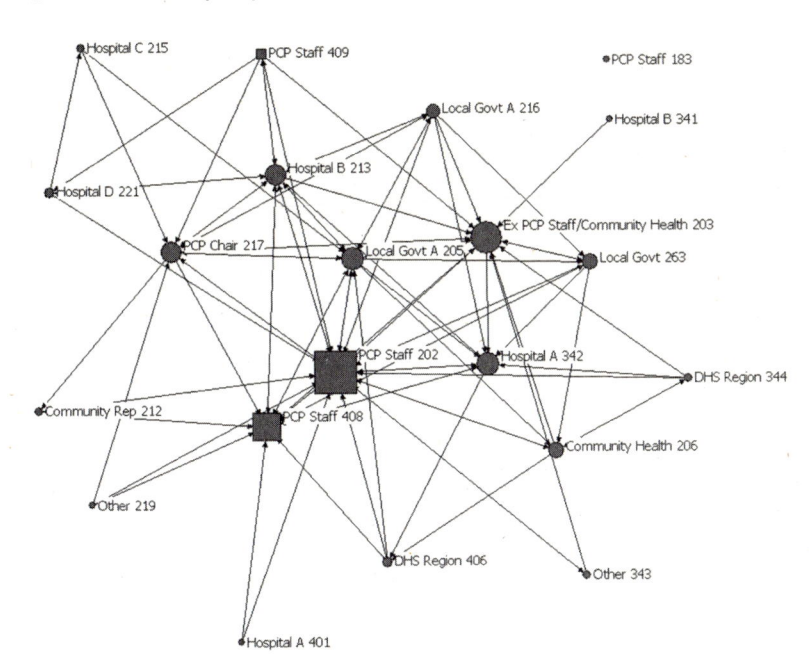

Figure 5.3 Campaspe work network, year 3

regional office. Only the person who took on the role of PCP Manager became more central; other prominent actors in the first year became less central. This signifies a broadening of the range of actors that respondents nominated as important, as well as the continuing prominence of partnership staff.

The pattern for the second year of results is generally quite similar to the first (see Table 5.1). PCP representatives remain the most centrally placed in both networks for both partnerships, despite the departure of two key actors – the Campaspe PCP Manager and the original Chair of Westbay. A third departure, one that made a smaller impact, was of the original DHS person on the steering committee. Notably, the new Chair remains prominent in the network at Westbay. At Campaspe,

Partnerships • 145

the ranking of the PCP staff member who became the new PCP Manager reflects that new status. In the strategic information network, hospitals became more important in the second year for Campaspe, while Community Health and one of the Divisions of General Practice became more important at Westbay.

Having become more densely connected in the second year, in the third year the work network at Campaspe became more sparse, with the number of ties falling from 111 to 90 despite the number of actors remaining the same (Figure 5.3). Network turnover was again quite high, with six members changing. Three actors became especially central – the two PCP staff (one a new addition to the network), and a previous PCP staff member who was now employed in Community Health. Aside from these three, only five other actors received more than five ties from other respondents in the network – one from local government, two from different hospitals, and the PCP Chair. This pattern indicates a loosening of the network structure, but again, the continuing importance of partnership staff is striking.

For the final year of the study, more key changes had occurred at Campaspe. Most significantly, another of the original three PCP staff (202) now occupied the role of Manager, with the previous Manager having moved on to a new role in Community Health but maintaining a position on the steering committee of the PCP. At Westbay, the original PCP Manager was still in place, and another staff member had been appointed to replace the person who departed (46). This is similar to the previous years (see Table 5.1), with PCP staff still important in both partnerships, along with local government in Campaspe and Community Health in Westbay. In both partnerships, DHS has disappeared from the top five most central actors for both work and strategic information.

The centrality for organisations (Table 5.2) also changed over the three years. For Campaspe, respondents consistently nominated PCP staff most in the first year, with 38 per cent of all ties directed towards them. This figure declined substantially in the second year as the network diversified, but rose marginally in the third year. Local government representatives remained relatively central at Campaspe over the three years, while actors based in hospitals became more important – the percentage of ties to this group doubled to 20 per cent over three years. The sharp rise for Community Health reflects the movement of one former PCP staff member, as discussed earlier. Perhaps of most interest is the loss of centrality of DHS regional office personnel, falling from 19 per cent in Year 1 to just 3.3 per cent in Year 3.

The PCP staff at Westbay also rate consistently as the most highly nominated; this rose slightly over the three years of the study. Local government actors declined steeply in importance from the first to the second year, but recovered somewhat in the third year. The impact of an unsettling amalgamation of the relevant DHS regional office with a contiguous one is clear in the third year, with the centrality of this group falling to zero. The relative importance of the PCP Chair at Westbay is also clear from this Table, with the Chair ranging between 13 and 19 per cent over the three years, compared with between 6.1 and 7.8 per cent for Campaspe. Similarly, hospitals were less important at Westbay, varying from zero to 8.1 per cent, while at Campaspe, they scored between 10 and 20 per cent.

Partnership relationships

Those involved in partnerships are not simply passive points in a network structure: They are actively creating and sustaining relationships with others. This chapter now considers how those involved use and value their network ties.

Everybody interviewed in these two PCPs in the first year thought they had greater engagement with other agencies than prior to the PCP, and almost all saw this as positive. The Westbay CEO commented: 'We've got people around the table who haven't been around the table before … through the regular meetings and forums … you can eyeball someone and know who it is.' A less positive comment came from one (fairly peripheral) actor: 'I don't think that people have got time to waste … I think it's just quite cumbersome to go to meeting after meeting and run into the same people.' A telling comment on connections to the Divisions of General Practice was made by one interviewee at Campaspe:

> I've probably dealt more with the Division of GPs in the last six months than I have in the previous five years and, even though they have a strong relationship with a few hospitals, there was never a need or a perceived need to talk to them directly, but now that I've made the contacts I talk to them about lots of different things.

Comments about the quality of relationships revealed that most people valued the partnerships and were using them for a variety of purposes. Several spoke of how trust had been built through the PCPs, leading to opportunities to do more things together. One of the weakly linked peripheral people said: 'I think we're a lot better off, we're a lot better networked.' Campaspe's Chair said:

> I think it's about establishing networks. Because you know more people involved in different services, if something crosses your desk and it might be a funding application or whatever, if it rings bells you think, 'Oh yes, I could talk to so and so about that, that links in to this program and we could do so and so together.'

These comments from the first year of the partnerships highlight how relationships were developing through them. Interestingly, a number of people were using networks as a concept in their comments and some spoke in quite specific network or partnership terms (overcoming boundaries and cut-offs, more and better networking, developing relationships, working together, strengthening ties).

Over the three years of the study, many interviewees referred to relationships as having changed and strengthened because of PCPs. This comment was typical: 'I think the big achievement of Primary Care Partnerships is that they've moved us to a default position of cooperation.' A range of factors related to the use and value of these partnerships were raised by those who were interviewed. These mainly related to building relationships, engaging individual partner agencies, managing the collaborative process, the amount of direction and control from DHS, and funding issues. These were important throughout the three years, although the specific issues changed over time. Many respondents referred to relationships as having changed and strengthened over the three years, noting the benefits of the shift to a more collaborative model.

The interviewees' comments correspond to the network maps and measures reported above, reinforcing the importance of the PCP staff, and also of having someone *not* from one of the organisations in the partnerships doing the work of coordinating them. Despite this, some interviewees, particularly in later years, recognised that partnerships are not straightforward or easy. One respondent noted: 'I think partnerships are always going to be hard work. They always have a competitive edge. We're all running businesses and we all need for our businesses to survive.'

Another issue raised was the ongoing talk about balancing individual agency and the partnership agendas. One interviewee was particularly negative, claiming that since agencies would never put the joint interests of the PCP above the interests of their own agency, PCPs were therefore a failure: 'I said … "If we could come up with a service delivery model that improved the services to our community … and it impacted negatively on your agency, would you support it?" Everybody in the room said "No". Everybody.' This is in stark contrast to another respondent in the same partnership, who commented: 'I truly believe PCP is us … PCP is not external to us, we are PCP, we make PCP work for our community and our organisations.'

Comments about hospitals were often negative in the early years, particularly in relation to hospitals not seeing the point of getting involved, or thinking they are the major and most important health service provider in the area. The two PCPs had varying views on whether or not their engagement with hospitals had grown, with Campaspe being notably more positive. This is reflected in the higher centrality scores for hospital staff in the networks at Campaspe than in Westbay. Local government involvement was seen to be relatively poorly developed in the Westbay partnership, both in relation to people being uncertain whether local governments should have a major role, and in relation to them not being highly engaged. Again, this reflects their relatively low network centrality.

An obvious point where disengagement is likely to occur is GPs and the Divisions of General Practice, which are funded by the national government. GPs in Australia receive the vast majority of their funding on a fee-for-service basis, and have few financial incentives to become involved in partnership meetings and planning activities. Early comments reflected difficulty engaging the Division in the partnership. In later years, their role was spoken about in a more positive manner. However, the Divisions of General Practice do not feature as central in the networks for either PCP, even in the final year. One interviewee from Campaspe pointed to improved relations with both the Division and the Aboriginal Medical Service (AMS) as signs of PCPs working to overcome the boundaries between state-funded primary care activities and Commonwealth-funded general practice:

> I guess one of the organisations, in particular the AMS at Echuca, Njernda, and the Division [of General Practice] have got a much closer relationship and that was in fact, I guess, in some ways driven by PCP activities in the original phase and PCP personnel.

The need for specific funding for partnerships in order for them to work was raised often. With an initial three years of funding, and then an extension for another two years, it is not surprising that the issue of whether the funding for PCPs would continue was also raised frequently. Respondents noted the short-sightedness of the funding arrangements, and the impact of that: it undermined their trust in DHS and in each other. Many spoke about the importance of resources dedicated to the partnership work:

> [I]t's all very well having the will to work together, but you need [to have] some dedicated resources which are based solely on cooperation as opposed to everybody just having to make do within their own. It's much better. Concrete, resourced cooperation.

Some informants felt that the partnerships had become sufficiently embedded to enable important elements of the relationships to be sustained without continuing support:

> [T]here's been some really, really strong players and networks developed in the last 12 months [and], I think, if PCP funding was perhaps to be not ongoing, there would still be a really strong relationship there and we would be right.

Overall, the themes arising in the interviews largely reinforced the data on network structure and network dynamics. In particular, they point to the ongoing importance of PCP staff as network brokers, and to a diminution in the importance of direct links to the funding agency as the partnerships progressed.

In relation to the role of government, this analysis suggests that partnerships for this purpose (service coordination) require long-term support, not just start-up funding. The centrality of PCP staff in both partnerships and both kinds of network, and across the three years, indicates a need for independent (of partner agencies) and dedicated funding and support for network staff positions over a substantial period of time. However, if these positions were removed, it is possible that the networks would be rebuilt by others who were prepared to take on the coordination role in addition to their individual organisational role. Given the stretched resources of the many small organisations involved, however, it seems unlikely that this could be sustained. Also, having partnership brokers who are not affiliated with one particular organisation in the partnership is important: their organisational affiliation is seen to be primarily to the partnership rather than to one of the partners.

Community development partnerships

Social and economic restructuring over the past decades in Australia has adversely affected some communities, who have lost major assets in the shift away from manufacturing towards service and knowledge industries, experienced demographic change as their populations age or move to cities, or seen globalisation diminish control over their local circumstances (Howe & Cleary 2001). In recognition of this, over the past five years the Department of Planning and Community Development (DPCD) has been brokering partnerships that bring together government, NGOs, businesses and community members to identify and address such issues in specific geographic areas. These partnerships are one strategy within the broader social policy efforts of the Victorian Government's social policy agenda: *A Fairer Victoria* (State Government of Victoria 2008).

The DPCD's community development arm was established in 2002. Its aim was to strengthen communities by strengthening local governance arrangements, because there was a growing concern that governments were becoming distant from local communities and were difficult to navigate, complex, and sometimes uncoordinated. There was also increasing interest in the role of social capital and networks in community development and the potential role of governments in building networks. The department saw a need to engage communities in planning and civic life, and there was an increasing interest in ways governments could work in partnership with business and local communities in the planning and delivery of services (DPCD 2007).

The different types of partnerships that were established address socioeconomic disadvantage concentrated in particular geographic areas, socioeconomically disadvantaged population groups (such as Indigenous populations), and disadvantage related to a lack of services in new growth areas on the metropolitan fringe. The partnerships bring together a range of organisations concerned about these issues (Montgomery 2005).

This section of the chapter reports on research conducted in 2007 to examine how some of these partnerships were working and to draw out lessons about what made them function successfully. A more detailed version of this research can be found in Pope and Lewis (2008). In total, 10 partnerships were involved in this research. A summary of them, in terms of the partners involved, purpose, prior investment and funding for brokers, is provided in Table 5.3. For three of the ten partnerships in the study, the information collected was baseline information, as they were still primarily in a relationship-building phase. They are not included in the table.

All but one was instigated by DPCD in response to interest in an issue (the exception being the one initiated by the Council of Australian Governments). They are all voluntary, and none was formed as a condition for receiving resources beyond the broker. Just under half were created in sites where investment and energy had already been put into building a community or resident network. In each case, DPCD has provided support in the form of the broker – although in most the broker is jointly funded or supported by a partner agency in some way (for example, office and on-costs) (see Table 5.3). The partnerships' work plans are jointly funded by partners and other sources, such as competitive grants. The partnerships are self-governed and determine their own processes for operating. However, half are held accountable through performance criteria set by the Department rather than by the partnership.

Network structures

The approach here is similar to that taken for the PCPs, in that it combines an analysis of structure and of agency. Connections between people are examined through network mapping of relations. This is combined with an exploration of the quality of nships within partnerships. This involved interviewing up to 15 members of the partnership's steering committee (or equivalent governance body) in face-to-face or telephone interviews. In total, 120 people were interviewed.[5]

Interviewees were asked about: their relationships with each of the other partners; organisations or people that should have been involved but were not; the biggest successes or achievements that had resulted from the partnership (if any); what had helped and what had hindered their work; what could have been done better; what lessons they had learned that could be translated elsewhere; and the sustainability of the partnership activities or its outcomes. They were also asked to name the people they talked to most to undertake their day-to-day work in the partnership and to get strategic information about the partnership, using the same questions as for PCPs. The information provided in interviews was transcribed and grouped into themes. The respondent-generated effectiveness criteria, which arose from the themes that developed in the interviews, were used in an interactive way, along with the characteristics of effective partnerships identified in the literature.

The day-to-day work and strategic information network data were used to create maps for the partnerships, as was done for the PCPs examined above. However, the map shown in Figure 5.4 includes both interviewees and those mentioned by someone who was interviewed. As in previous maps, the arrowhead indicates the direction of the nomination (from whom to whom). Here the thicker lines indicate relationships that were signified as 'crucial'. People who were nominated but not interviewed are around the edges of this map.

Table 5.3 Community development partnerships: key characteristics

Partnership, partners and purpose	Prior investment	Broker funded by	Research undertaken
The Caroline Springs Partnership Melton Shire Council, Delfin Lend Lease and DPCD Trialled a new way of planning and delivering infrastructure and services in a new development in a growth area	State-funded education services broker was previously assisting in developing education infrastructure and services	Developer, council, state government	Final evaluation After 15 months' operation (project complete)
The Aboriginal Council of Australian Governments (COAG) Partnership in Shepparton Local, state and Federal government and a coalition of Indigenous organisations and representatives Examining ways to improve the social and economic wellbeing of the Aboriginal community and support cultural sustainability	COAG	State and Federal government, administrative support from local government	Interim evaluation In its 4th year, but only first since Aboriginal Policy Unit established to help community participate
Laverton Community Renewal Local and state government, NGOs and residents Examining ways to revitalise an outer suburb through economic development, housing improvements, neighbourhood precinct renewal and improved governance	Builds on previous DPCD-funded community engagement activities	State government, administrative support from local government	Interim evaluation In its 2nd year
Transport Connections Partnerships (3 included in study) Local and state government, NGOs, community members, transport providers and local business Examining ways to develop transport solutions tailored to communities' needs	None	State government, administrative support from local government (2) and a volunteer agency (1)	Interim evaluation In its 4th year
Wimmera Regional Sports Assembly Local and state government and health and sporting NGOs Examining ways to support and build the capacity of sporting groups and clubs in the region	None	State government, administrative support from local government	Interim evaluation In its 25h year (ongoing work)

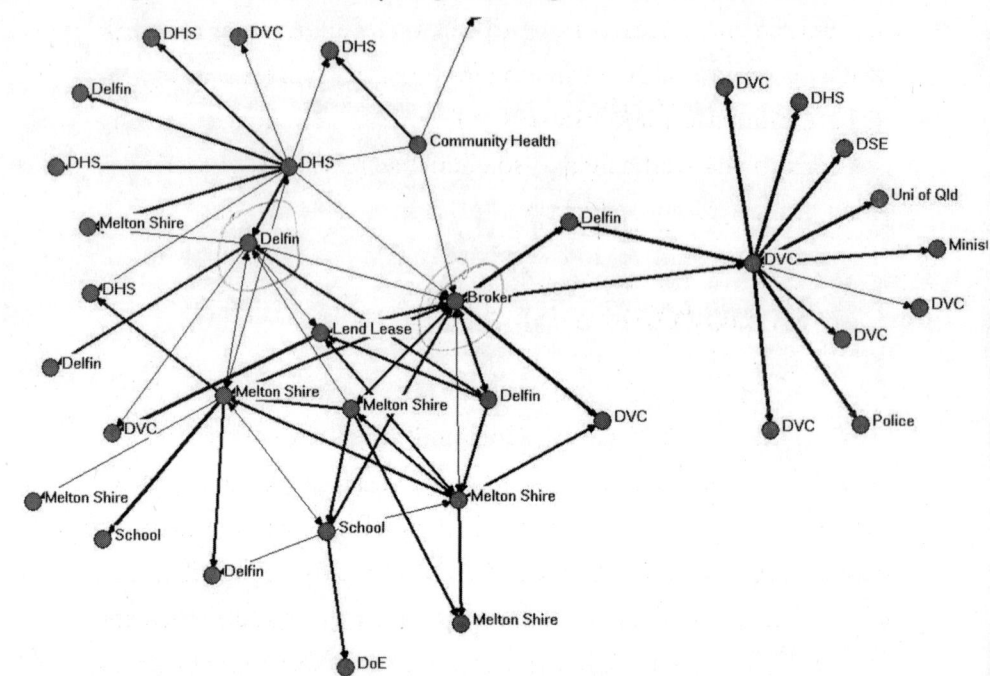

Figure 5.4 Caroline Springs strategic information network

Analysis of the interview responses revealed a limited number of characteristics that were features of all the effective partnerships. Conversely, the absence of these features was reported as hindering some of the new partnerships. The characteristics were generally in line with those reported in the literature. They are: a good broker/facilitator to build relationships; decision makers at the table who had a commitment and the authority to contribute; a clear purpose; good partnership processes; and ongoing motivation through champions and evaluation. A detailed description of these five factors can be found in Pope and Lewis (2008). Only the first of these is reviewed in detail here, as it highlights the characteristics that are most important for networks and social capital building in terms of the framework of this book. The maps of network structures were important for partnerships wanting to examine their interactions with others in order to identify strong connections as well as gaps, so their use is also discussed.

The importance of brokers

The first factor, a good broker, was reported as the main thing that helped all partnerships. Conversely, some partnerships reported that the absence of a good broker was the main thing that had hindered their work. The brokers are easy to identify in the network maps, because they are highly nominated and centrally placed. This is similar to the pattern that emerged for the PCPs. The partnership literature details the importance of brokers and the relationship building they undertake (Skelcher et al. 1996; Mandell 2001; Provan & Milward 2001; Keast et al. 2004). When partners first come together they do not necessarily see themselves as interdependent. To achieve this requires building an understanding of other organisations. The success of partnerships is therefore dependent on relationship building, which involves people learning about each other and reshaping their views (Mandell 2002–03). The reshaping of views about others was apparent in the partnerships in this study. Many of those interviewed reported their partnership's biggest achievement had been bringing people together across departments and organisations and learning about how others operate. This strengthened understanding between organisations, broke down stereotypes, and made partners more aware of the constraints other organisations face.

Brokers were described as critical in the process of relationship building but were also described as useful because they fostered cooperation, kept an eye on the work and made sure that everything was completed, provided the partnerships with capacity that they otherwise lacked, assisted in navigating the state bureaucracy, and identified opportunities and resources. The skills and experience of successful brokers were: communication, networking, facilitation and negotiation skills; project management skills; local knowledge and some standing in the community; knowledge of the workings of state and local government; independence from the partners (owned by all partners); and being highly personable and enthusiastic.

Brokers were also reported as useful in keeping things moving, and in dealing with some of the obstacles to the partnerships, including blockers (organisations or individuals that slowed down partnership activity or acted against the interests of the partnership), staff turnover (particularly in the state and Federal bureaucracies), and organisational silos (especially in governments at each level).

The importance of brokers is neatly illustrated by the network map in Figure 5.4, which shows the strategic information network for the Caroline Springs Partnership. Partners reported that relationships were stormy between the council and the developer, and non-existent with state government (except with the then Department of Education) before the partnership (DPCD 2007). All organisations reported that their relationships had improved enormously – to the point where there was now a large amount of trust and confidence in, and understanding of, each other – and that this was largely the result of the broker.

A well-connected local network has been created, as shown to the left of Figure 5.4, which includes local government, regional state government agencies, Delfin Lend Lease, local schools and some NGOs. The state government broker can be seen on the right edge of the left-hand cluster. This broker links the local network to a range of other state government decision makers, including three central departments and the Minister responsible for planning. Again, the broker is connected to others predominantly through dark lines, because the relationship was perceived by all steering committee members to be critical. This broker has since been removed (as the project was complete), leaving behind a strong local partnership that is moving on to new infrastructure development projects in the area. It will need to foster links with outside agencies to replace those that existed through the broker. The partnership became aware of this by examining the network maps. This was part of the interactive design used: the maps were fed back to the partnerships' brokers and steering committees so they could see the structure of their partnership and examine the role of their organisation within it. Using the maps from the study, the brokers and partnerships were encouraged to discuss the following questions:

1 Whose voices are included and are these the right people/groups to address the problem? Who does not speak to people back in their home organisation?

2. Have relationships been strengthening over time?
3. Which organisations that are vital to the success of the work have tenuous links? Who is not involved but should be? Should involvement be broadened/limited?
4. Who has links to important resources and decision makers? If someone left, what links to external decision makers would be lost? How sustainable are the relationships over time?
5. How is the partnership linked to the democratic institutions of government and to the community of interest? Are there capacity issues for the community in being involved? (see Pope & Lewis 2008).

Examining these questions about where additional relationship building was necessary ensured that a range of crucial partnership issues was discussed.

Conclusions

The ideal characteristics of partnerships, presented earlier in this chapter, are a useful tool with which to examine structures and untangle relationships. Partnerships require time and resources to become established and then build social capital for those involved in them, as well as for their clients. Network concepts and network maps and measures can answer some important evaluative questions about partnerships, before the longer term effects of partnerships are realised. The application of them here has helped describe partnership configurations, and track structures and dynamics over time. Combined with a narrative about how they are valued, this provides a powerful means of evaluation.

The ideal characteristics of well-connected core partners – very central brokers, ongoing centrality of the brokers over time, low centrality of the funding agency, a reasonable level of redundancy, positive evaluations of the relationships, and a sense that they will be sustainable with continuing funding (for PCPs) or with new arrangements (for community development) – help uncover the level of 'success' of the networks concerned. The benefits of these attempts to build social capital by increasing connections and improving relationships between organisations should flow to organisations and their clients (in the case of the health partnerships) and to local communities (in the case of the community development partnerships).

A network-centred approach such as the one outlined in this chapter provides insights into network structures and how actors are using them to strengthen relationships. It also provides the partnerships with a useful diagnostic tool so that they can direct their energy to shaping future operations in ways that are most likely to lead to strong structures and effective partnerships. This approach captures important attributes of partnerships: those involved in such partnerships need to know this so that the partnerships can generate social capital to improve services or to build communities. Alongside achievements and outcomes, this provides a robust method for making claims about the outcomes of policy interventions whose purpose is to build social capital.

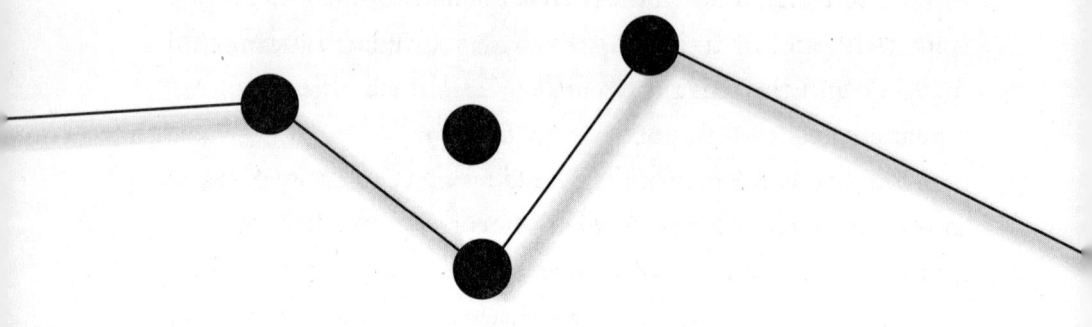

6 Knowledge

Knowledge generation has been high on the agenda of Australian and other nations' governments for some time. Increasing attention has been directed to encouraging the formation of research networks through collaborative grants of various kinds. The Australian Research Council (ARC) and the National Health and Medical Research Council (NHMRC) offer a growing range of collaborative grants that provide incentives for people to work with others. The ARC offers linkage grants, which encourage academics to find industry partners who are interested in contributing funding to research they are interested in, research network grants, which encourage academics from around Australia and the world to form loose coalitions around shared topics of interest, and Centre of Excellence grants, which are also multi-institutional and have links to non-academic organisations. The NHMRC has program grants that support large numbers of academics over extended periods of time, and more recently has introduced partnership grants which, like ARC linkages, involve industry partners. All of these are predicated on an assumption that funds spent on collaboration will pay dividends in terms of knowledge generation. The Federal Government also funds cooperative research centres (multi-institution centres that involve large numbers of people), and there are many other funds that also encourage collaboration.

Doing research with others might be the ultimate form of producing social capital. Academics working together – getting grants for projects together, working on things of mutual interest, and writing publications together – is at first blush very much a self-organising activity. Academic work can be a solitary activity, but when academics form networks, they choose who they will do research with and are able to link up with others who have shared intellectual interests. However, while a degree of autonomy is certainly at play, there are several other factors that help shape who works together and in what sorts of configurations. As indicated already, one of these is government policy, as it determines what types of collaboration attract funding.

Academic networks are also shaped by 'how things are done' in different disciplines, and by the habits that individual academics have developed during years of study and then taken into their work as academics. The solo researcher toiling away by him/herself is reasonably common in the humanities, but it can be argued that this is a model that is losing purchase as policy increasingly encourages collaboration rather than solo work.

Social scientists tend to work more with others, and scientists working in large laboratories would never contemplate working on a project by themselves. Multidisciplinary areas of research are (obviously) collaborative, since a range of disciplines and skills are required to do the work. These different models of working flow through into publishing. There are myriad informal rules, traditions and values that determine who has his/her name on a publication (as well as the order in which the names appear), and these also vary widely from discipline to discipline, impacting on who does research together.

An important aspect of this, in terms of network structures, is the distinction between concrete collaborations, which are clearly signalled by co-authored publications and multi-investigator grants, and the more expressive networks. Not all academics have the first of these, but even those who solo author every publication have discussions with colleagues (these may be close by or far away), and will interact with interested others at conferences and seminars. In relation to both of these, we want to know first, whether or not there is a network, and second, if there is, how large it is.

There are some other important structural factors of interest in this case. It is important, when examining academic networks (and all the other networks analysed in this book), to think about what resources these networks provide access to. Certainly there is intellectual capital to be had, through connections to other smart people with good ideas. But there is also support for early career researchers, trying to find their way in a highly competitive environment. Connections to other academics can also help generate desirable outcomes such as successful grant applications;

some of these might have failed if presented as sole investigator projects. This case is ripe with possibilities for analysing the networks that matter and how they are structured, the social capital they might produce for academics, and what government and individual institutions' policies can do to help individuals and groups form and use these links to create new knowledge.

It is clear that academic networks provide access to resources. But in this case, as in the others, these networks are not necessarily based on trust and shared norms. Academics can form networks for instrumental purposes, such as to attract grants. There are powerful incentives to work with others that have little to do with personal affiliation or shared values and more to do with benefits that might flow from cooperation. Shared values might make collaboration easier, but it is possible for groups to work together when those involved have different values, and there are many collaborations where having shared values or liking each other is considered irrelevant to the research.

Social capital in this case is centred on individuals, with their ties to other researchers representing the potential to generate new knowledge and with publications as the outputs. Successfully working on a project and publishing together feeds back into strengthening relationships and increases the chances that actors will collaborate again. And the reverse is of course true too. Failed collaborations ensure that the actors will move on and find others to work with. In academic networks, as in all other networks, power is an issue: senior academics are able to coopt junior researchers because they can significantly influence the junior researchers' future careers – either positively or negatively. Academic networks might produce lively forums with free-flowing discussion, and generate career benefits to their members, but they can certainly have their dark side, and they are by no means sites where everyone is equal.

The main social network concept to be explored in research networks is proximity. Proximity to other academics with whom fruitful exchanges can be enjoyed is one of the crucial requirements of successful collaboration. Dialogue is more difficult across disciplinary distances, for example. But heterophily also has a positive side, as the robustness of an idea must be questioned if it has not been tested beyond a small circle of like-minded individuals. As with all the other cases in this book, it is the pattern and quality of connections that matter most to social capital generation and to producing desired outcomes, such as new knowledge. This second case of a policy prescription to generate social capital – in this case the platform underpinning new knowledge generation – focuses on a specific group of people and institutions (researchers, universities, research institutes, companies with large R&D arms, and any organisation with an interest in being involved in research), unlike the previous chapter, in which the interventions were targeted on geographic areas.

Three levels that shape academic networks

The idea of building social capital in this area begins from the assumption that networks of various types are an important part of the research process. As this book has already argued at some length, networks are crucial in gaining information, building alliances, and accessing resources. Clearly, there are tensions between what national policy funds, what disciplinary colleagues value, and what leads academics to do research together. Hence there are three levels of analysis required for this case. First, the institutional context signals which research outputs attract funding. This sets notional boundaries around how academics establish networks and do research. Second, disciplinary traditions shape academic networks and guide what is valued by peers (this may or may not align well with what is funded by governments). Third, academics generate networks through intellectual curiosity and shared research interests. These three levels interact, producing a range of signals about the value of making connections. These signals reinforce or conflict with research policy to varying extents, according to the level of congruence between policy, disciplinary traditions and individual preferences.

Universities are embedded in their country's policy context, and this of course affects academic work. Many operate within a public policy framework of 'academic capitalism' that values both profit and academic prestige (Slaughter & Leslie 1997). Knowledge may be a goal in itself, but the research context may also focus on manufacturing products ... the more, the faster, the better (Fuller 2000). In Australia, prestige is substantially related to research success – measured in grants and publications – which feeds back into the level of funding that universities receive from government. Research policy shapes the signals that research managers send to academics about which activities are valued and how academics should work (with colleagues in other disciplines, with international colleagues, with industry, and so on). In academia, the last decades have witnessed an increasing emphasis on targets, competition, and the use of auditing and performance indicators – such as linking funding to measurable research outputs that are seen to represent knowledge generation.

Research cultures vary across disciplines. Friedkin's (1998) landmark research on the physical, biological and social sciences at Columbia University and the University of Chicago showed that interpersonal networks between academics were crucial in coordinating academic work, and that the structure of these networks varied across disciplines and universities, with high levels of interaction and collaboration between a small number of groups and across disciplines in some cases (physical science at Columbia), much more complicated and balanced patterns in others (biological science at Columbia), and little interaction across disciplines in others (social science at both universities).

This chapter assumes that a number of different networks produce social capital. It also assumes that only some networks result in joint grants and co-authorship. Co-authorship is often used as the pre-eminent marker of collaboration (see Rigby & Edler 2005; Wagner & Leydesdorff 2005). It is used as a proxy measure of outcomes (or effects) here to illustrate the substantial differences among disciplines. While publications are certainly one verifiable indicator of which actors are working together, they are not the only one. Other indicators that are less easy to track, such as being in a research group together or discussing research with someone but not publishing with them, appear to be crucial in some disciplines, as this chapter demonstrates.

Information on the publication networks that follows suggests that different kinds of networks appear in different parts of the academy.

After mapping publication networks in different disciplines, this chapter examines how academics in the humanities and social sciences value and use their networks, and how these networks might benefit from collaborative research funding. Interviews with these academics, who work in fields where collaboration is less common, at least in the sense of concrete outcomes (publications), were used to do this.

Publication networks

To highlight disciplinary differences, publications data for the Faculties of Arts and Science at the University of Melbourne, over the period 2001–05, was analysed. The first analysis is of the volume of multi-authored publishing. Table 6.1 provides information on the number of single and multi-authored books, book chapters, journal articles and refereed conference papers (the four kinds of publications that attract government funds) from 2001 to 2005. The difference between the faculties is striking: over this five-year period, 21 per cent of book chapters from Arts had more than one author, compared with 86 per cent for Science. This pattern is similar for journal articles (19 per cent for Arts, 96 per cent for Science) and conference papers (30 per cent compared with 92 per cent). This highlights some different disciplinary practices in these two faculties, which are in the one university, in regard to authorship practices.

Table 6.1 Single and multi-authored publications

	Arts		Science	
	Single author	Multi-authored	Single author	Multi-authored
Books	174	23	3	2
% more than one author		13%		40%
Book chapters	556	147	23	145
% more than one author		21%		86%
Journal articles	1031	242	232	5073
% more than one author		19%		96%
Conference papers	152	66	69	775
% more than one author		30%		92%

Table 6.1 also indicates the differences in volume of different publication types. In 2001–05, Arts Faculty academics published 197 research books, 703 book chapters, 1273 journal articles and 218 conference papers. Science academics spend far more of their energy on journal articles and conference papers, and less on books. They published only five research books in this five-year period, and 168 book chapters. However, 5305 journal articles and 844 conference papers were published.

A second analysis is provided by a network map of journal articles published in 2005 for these two faculties, shown in Figures 6.1 and 6.2. In these figures, each dot is a person, and in this case, each line indicates a co-author relationship. There are no arrowheads indicating who nominates whom or who goes to whom for some purpose, as these are undirected ties. The thickness of the line varies with the number of co-authored publications (thicker lines indicate more co-authored publications). Colours indicate departments, and white indicates someone external to the Arts Faculty. Every person in a cluster has not necessarily published with all the others. Where each dot is joined to all others in a cluster, then all these people have published together.

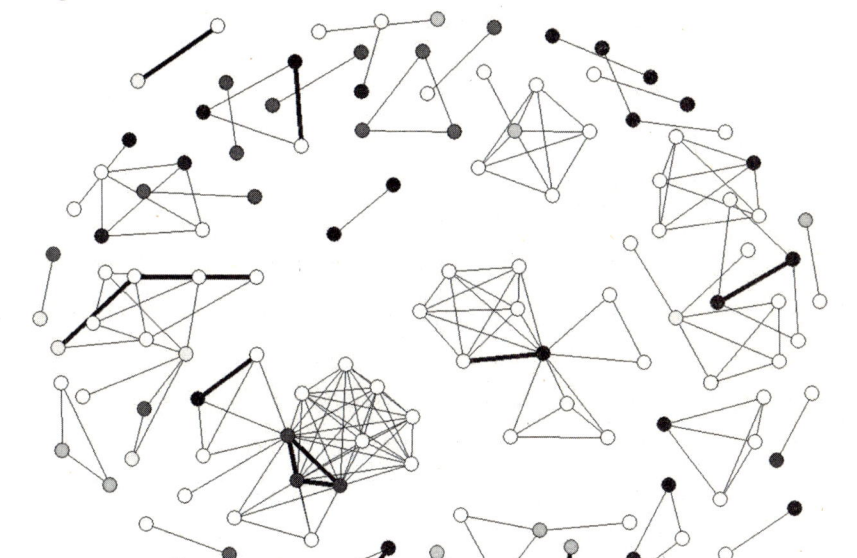

Figure 6.1 Arts multi-authored articles

The network map in Figure 6.1 shows that a common configuration in the Arts faculty is to publish with one or two other people; there are only a small number of clusters with more than three authors. Figure 6.2 shows the much larger groups of people co-authoring papers in the sciences. Although it is not easy to observe from these maps, especially the complicated

Knowledge • 173

and large map for Science, there are also differences in terms of the location of co-authors. In Arts the most common pattern is to co-author with someone else from the same department, or with someone from outside the university. In Science there is far more co-authoring with people from different departments and different faculties within this university, as well as a substantial amount of co-authoring with academics from elsewhere.

To further illustrate the differences in these networks, this time at the individual level, the ego network for publications in 2005 for two different people in very different disciplines are shown in Figures 6.3 and 6.4. In these figures the larger circles indicate the person whose publishing network this is. Thicker lines indicates more joint publications, and the different shapes indicate different departments in the university as well as actors from outside the university, so the circles indicate actors from the same department as the person whose network this is. Figure 6.3 is the network map for a political scientist, who had one publication with two other people in this year; his other publications were sole-authored. One of these people is in the same department and the other is at another university. Figure 6.4 is the publishing network of a radiologist, which shows that she bridges across two domains and five departments.

These two extremes illustrate the differences between the publication networks of people in different parts of the academy. They reflect disciplinary practices, and provide grounds to claim that a new policy emphasis on collaborative research would relatively advantage the radiologist, who is already accustomed to working with many others.

Figure 6.2 Science multi-authored articles

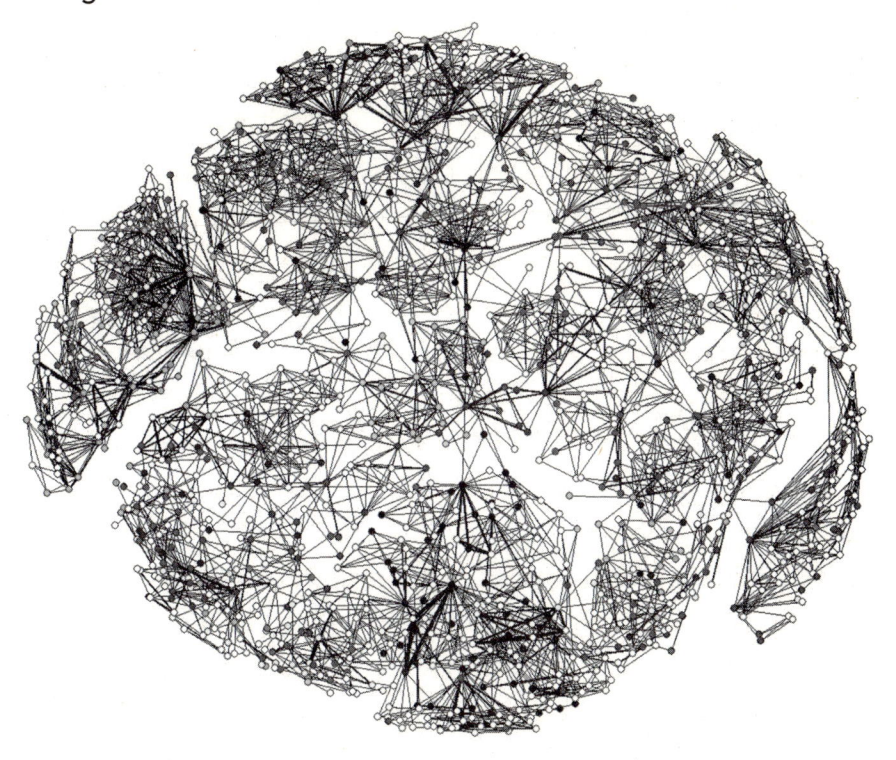

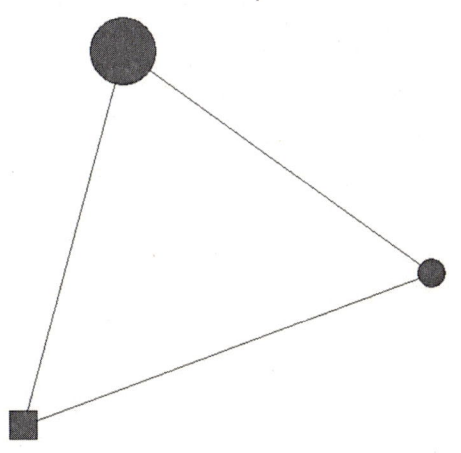

Figure 6.3 Publication network for a political scientist

Knowledge • 175

Figure 6.4 Publication network for a radiologist

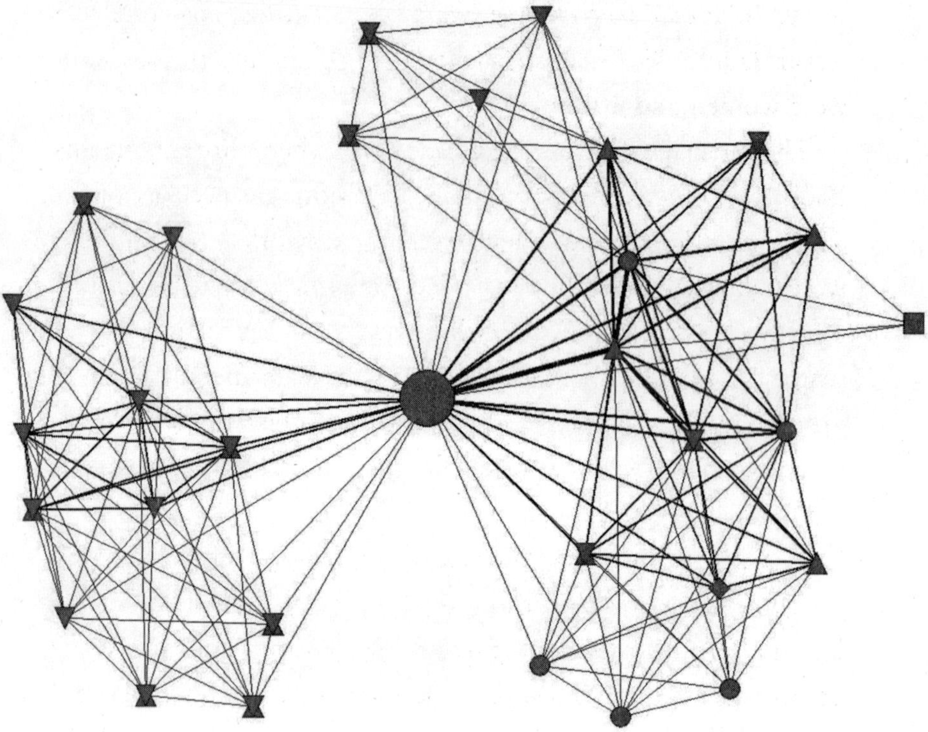

Research networks

Interviews with academics in the Faculty of Arts were conducted in 2007. This faculty covers history, archaeology and classics, languages and linguistics, literature, media and communications, philosophy, anthropology, criminology, geography, political science and sociology. A total of 36 interviews were conducted. Lecturers and Associate Professors were targeted, to obtain views from more junior and senior staff. Coverage across the disciplines was achieved by approaching people from various schools within the faculty. Invitations were sent to 83 academics – 50 lecturers and 33 Associate Professors. Of these, 36 agreed to participate (a 43 per cent response rate): 23 lecturers and 13 Associate Professors. Of the interviewees, 16 were women and 20 were men.

The interviews in this study, as in the others throughout this book, contained specific network questions, as well as open-ended questions about their research networks. Interviewees were asked whether they regarded themselves as being part of a research group or cluster either within the university or elsewhere. They were then asked to describe what people in these groups had in common and the activities they engaged in together, and to discuss any benefits they thought came from being involved in such a group.

Few people in the faculty felt they were in a strong research group or cluster within the university, with more referring to external groups they were part of. This did not appear to vary greatly across disciplines, or by career stage. Of those who did see themselves as being in an internal group, many saw that as based simply on having a disciplinary background in common, and others said it was because they had a common research interest. Many saw themselves as being in an internal group 'only in a fairly weak way'.

Of those who identified with some internal group (even a very informal one), the most frequently mentioned kinds of activities engaged in were team teaching and supervision, organising conferences and seminars, participating in reading groups and discussion groups, participating in informal social events, and reading drafts of other people's work. External group activities mentioned frequently were conference organisation, and working on edited books and themed special issues of journals with colleagues. A small number of interviewees identified publishing together as a group activity, but more spoke about writing grant applications together as an activity of their research group.

People identified a range of benefits that accrued from their internal research networks, which can be summarised into: intellectual encouragement, criticism and support; personal support and mentoring (especially for early career researchers); and improving research outcomes. In the first cluster, people mentioned peer encouragement, motivation, sharing ideas, cross-fertilisation of ideas, getting constructive feedback, and reducing intellectual isolation. As one person said: 'The peer review process reinforces ideology and dogma, and stifles creative thinking. Being in a supportive research group helps.' Some mentioned feeling a collective sense of purpose, or being part of an intellectual community as benefits, and others emphasised the benefits of working with people outside academia. Early career researchers talked more about personal support, mentoring, building contacts, and learning from more experienced academics.

The benefits identified in regard to strengthening research outcomes were: being more productive in producing publications; being more successful in winning grants; and being able to bring people with different skills together to strengthen grant applications. The link to activities that attract funding, and the increased emphasis being placed on collaboration, was clearly articulated by those who were interviewed. In addition to the questions about research networks, people were asked whether they tended to publish alone, or with others, or both, and to discuss why. They were also asked whether they tended to apply for grants alone, or with others, or both, and why.

A substantial number of the interviewees said that they only publish alone, but almost as many said that they publish both alone and with others. Discussion about why varied across the disciplines, but this was also related to career stage, with more junior researchers having only published alone so far. Most people indicated that they applied for grants both alone and with others. The responses here seemed to differ more by career stage than by discipline, but there were some clear patterns related to disciplines. Discussion about approaches and methods also related strongly to disciplines.

People publish alone for a number of reasons that relate to their discipline, including because it's the nature of the discipline to be solitary and private, and that they are part of a discipline that has an individualistic research culture. The following comments are examples of this: 'the discipline doesn't lend itself to collaboration', or it is just 'the way we work in humanities'. Others gave more personal reasons, such as it suits the way they work, they like to be autonomous, that to publish together you need to agree on absolutely everything, or that they are not close to others who focus on the same topic, and that 'you need to trust others' scholarship to collaborate'. Across the disciplines, a number of people identified the reasons for solo publishing as relating to being in a highly specialist field, saying that there are no 'natural research colleagues' here or elsewhere who are expert in the same field, that their interest is so narrow that there is no one to share with, or that there are no others with similar views. Others simply saw publishing with others as messy and solo publishing as easier. The majority of these comments came from people who identified themselves as historians, but people from other disciplines sometimes mentioned these discipline-based and personal reasons for solo publishing.

A number of early career researchers indicated that they had only published alone to date because they were publishing from their PhD theses, but that they expected to collaborate in the future. Many thought solo publishing was more efficient and more valued. Joint publishing was seen as counting less, in terms of both getting points (this refers to publications that attract funding) and being promoted. A typical comment was: 'Co-authoring takes twice as long and you receive half the credit.' Another interviewee noted: 'You can't be seen to ride on others' coat tails; you have to publish alone.' This feeling was more pronounced in the humanities than in the social sciences, but people right across the faculty expressed these concerns about co-authorship.

Those who said they publish with others said they did so because they find single authorship too solitary, or (for early career researchers) it helps them get published, or because they are doing interdisciplinary work that requires input from a range of perspectives. Some said they published with others simply because they work with others and so it makes sense to publish together.

Applying for grants with others is far more widely seen as a good idea than publishing together is. The main reasons mentioned in support of collaborative grants were instrumental: it improves the chances of success, and the sheer amount of work involved in applying was better split over a group of participants. A number of people mentioned that they apply for small grants alone, but you need collaborators for big grants, because there is a belief that grants are increasingly being awarded to teams. Again, early career researchers identified the benefits of joining up with more senior and experienced academics to improve their chances of success, and conversely, a few more senior academics noted that there could be 'outcomes for others' through joint grant applications.

Some people said they have only applied for grants by themselves to date, because they have 'no network' with others in the area. Only a few people mentioned interdisciplinary work as a reason to collaborate on grants, and only one mentioned that there are other (less directly instrumental) benefits: 'grants concretise relationships', and provide 'a good way of finding out if you can work together'.

Those interviewed recognise a set of disciplinary and cultural incentives that value individual scholarship in the humanities and (to a lesser extent) in the social sciences. They also receive strong messages that they need to apply for grants, and they need to do so with others in order to succeed. This disjunction between being part of a team in order to have grant success, and being disadvantaged because of being a team player if you are successful in publishing with others, neatly illustrates the interaction of the three levels discussed at the beginning of this chapter. It is clear that intellectual curiosity, disciplinary traditions and performance frameworks are all important in shaping how academics value and use networks.

Encouraging collaboration

There seem to be conflicting signals that academics in this faculty are receiving about the increased need to collaborate and the disciplinary traditions that encourage individualism in some parts of the academy. What should be done, in policy terms, to encourage networks that will generate social capital for those involved, and contribute to new knowledge? As reported earlier, recent Federal Governments have provided substantial incentives for academics to collaborate within and outside their home institutions and with non-academics. Much of this is regarded by those interviewed in this study as supporting a 'science model' of research, one that relies on teamwork and large projects, and it certainly fits more closely with the output networks for science (Figure 6.2) than for arts (Figure 6.1). Given the growing funding incentives to collaborate, what can be done to encourage collaboration in areas of academia where the traditional way of working is solo?

Participants in this study were asked what their faculty and the university should do to encourage collaboration, particularly in relation to building research groups. Many argued that more resources would encourage internal (to the university) collaborations: having more (non-academic) staff to help build collaborations, more resources for meetings with colleagues in other schools and other faculties, providing more small grants for internal collaborations, and setting up a register of researchers and their interests to make it easier to find potential collaborators were suggested. A number of initiatives to build external collaborations were mentioned too, including cross-institutional collaborative grants, funding for conferences, grants to bring international researchers to Melbourne, and more travel grants so that international collaborations could be strengthened. Having specific grants to help build collaborations with non-academic institutions was raised by a number of people. Early career researchers thought more resources should be directed to nurturing new groups and more junior researchers 'instead of funding established groups'. Some saw a need for a better means of splitting grants across schools and faculties. Others noted a need for support and training to help people establish and work in teams.

Several said the most helpful approach would be having more time to spend on research instead of on getting funds: 'Money isn't the issue; I need time.' These comments were part of a theme about non-financial obstacles to collaboration, which in turn related to what has traditionally been rewarded. People spoke about a lack of support for collaboration in terms of promotion, and a need to have a quantitative measure of collaboration and to factor it into workloads. There was a widespread feeling that there is 'nothing in our workload that says research collaboration is important or valued'. Time for collaboration should be protected and counted: 'If we are doing the work and the work is important, it should be recognised.' Others spoke about non-financial incentives that would encourage collaboration, such as prizes, and celebrating successes with informal events.

A number of people felt that there needed to be clearer signals that collaboration was valued. Some thought a university statement on collaborative research would be useful. Others thought it needed a mind shift, to an 'open-minded recognition of other disciplines', or a 'move beyond traditional notions of research'.

The responses to the question about supporting research networks were wrapped up with a discussion that was underway at the time of the interviews about the Howard Government's planned introduction of a new research funding system. This Research Quality Framework (RQF) was to allocate funds to research clusters, based on the quality of research outputs. The clusters were to be smaller than departments and schools but larger than individuals. At the time of the interviews, the university was engaged in allocating people to clusters based on disciplinary codes and other criteria. As a result, many expressed fears that they would be forced into clusters without any clear rationale, and that: 'Being put into groups and measured as a group won't lead to collaboration.' All interviewees thought clusters needed to be self-selected, bottom-up, and voluntary. As one person said, 'If it's just one more thing to do it's a burden and something the faculty wants rather than what we want ourselves.'

Early career researchers were concerned that they would be left out of the RQF exercise (and therefore clusters), as not everyone was to be included in the assessment. They thought this would be detrimental for their careers. While some thought clusters should be built around senior academics, others disliked this approach, which they thought would marginalise early career researchers, and women with career interruptions. Others, who regarded their work as multidisciplinary, were concerned about how they would fit into a single cluster. While some interviewees were concerned about the imposition of a 'science model' – meaning that everyone would be forced to work in teams – others thought much could be learned from colleagues in the sciences on this front.

Other suggestions for creating clusters that were less directly related to concerns about the RQF were about organising forums to present ideas and find out what others are doing, and encouraging interschool clusters and interfaculty clusters, and encouraging more non-academic external links. Some pointed to the need for serious consideration of how clusters would impact on the tradition of individual research and authorship. But some thought there would be positives because, as one person put it, 'Everyone here is separated and secretive about their research.'

Proximity

In academia, as elsewhere, networks provide access to valuable resources, and academics face a range of both constraints and opportunities in terms of forming these relationships. This chapter now moves on to examine the use of networks in academia, by focusing on disciplines and other important proximity measures in shaping network structures.

Academics form interpersonal networks of different kinds for a variety of purposes. As was noted earlier in this chapter, there are a number of organising principles at work here (curiosity, disciplinary traditions and performance frameworks), and they affect the formation of research networks, their use, and the outcomes that they produce. How are these research networks structured? Which factors are the most important in shaping them?

At the beginning of this chapter, I stated an assumption that research networks, based on discussions and sharing ideas, are important in generating new knowledge. Many factors shape and constrain these networks. The concept of proximity as an underlying factor in the patterning of resource linkages in networks helps here. Proximity in physical, economic and social space, and homophily, are expected to play important roles in the formation of research networks. Since social interactions tend to take place among individuals who are similar, homophily in academia, as the comments in the last section indicate, relates to disciplinary areas and location as well as to sentiment-based forms of closeness such as shared values.

A focus on social capital makes visible the fact that everyone has a different set of ties, and thus a different and particular capacity to access resources through these ties. The interest here is in examining these research network ties.

Network ties between people reflect organisational structures and processes as well as social norms and the attributes of individuals. Spontaneous ties are likely to form on the basis of affinities of various types, such as gender, age, and shared interests (McPherson & Smith-Lovin 1987). This tendency towards homophily is, of course, tempered by opportunities to form such ties. Work settings provide opportunities to link up with others who are at different levels in the organisation, or who have various interests, and also constrain these interactions through the structural features of the organisation. For example, senior women's networks within organisations are less homophilous than men's (Ibarra 1997), which at least partly reflects the lack of availability of peers of the same gender. Further, men's networks are more homophilous regardless of the reason for the tie, while women tend to seek advice and influence from men, but information and social support from women (Ibarra 1992).

Academics were asked to provide information on their expressive networks, defined as people they discussed their research interests and ideas with the most. For each person nominated, a series of proximity questions was asked: about physical location, discipline, academic level, gender, and whether the interviewee regarded each of these people as a colleague or as a colleague and a personal friend. The 36 people interviewed generated 233 ties to alters. The distribution of research network ties by these measures of proximity is shown in Table 6.2.

The largest proportion of ties was external to the university. Ties to others in the same department were the next most frequent, followed by those in the same faculty, then elsewhere in the university. The vast majority of ties were to people of the same disciplinary background and the same gender, and most ties were to people at higher academic levels than the nominator. Finally, ties were fairly evenly split on personal closeness, but more than half of them were to people seen to be friends as well as colleagues.

Based on this relatively small sample, we can see that geographical proximity is not important to research networks – these interviewees are most likely to reach outside their home institution in their networks. Where they do have colleagues in the university, they tend to be in the same department. The areas of most clearly homophilous ties are discipline and gender. The propensity to nominate people at higher levels probably reflects the fact that more than half the interviewees were

Table 6.2 Proximity of research network ties

Respondents	Ties	Percentage
Location	Same department	22.3
	Same faculty	12.9
	Elsewhere U of M	6.0
	External	58.8
Discipline	Same	63.5
	Different	34.3
	Non-academic	2.1
Academic level	Higher	61.1
	Same	21.2
	Lower	17.8
Gender	Same	62.7
	Different	37.3
Colleague/friend	Colleague only	40.3
	Friend and colleague	59.7

lecturers, whose ties are most likely to be either upwards or sideways. Personal closeness is very split.

However, we cannot impute reasons behind the formation and use of ties from this data. This area was explored by asking interviewees about the perceived benefits they receive from being in research networks. The question was open-ended, and the information generated was grouped into five main themes, shown in Table 6.3. Two of the themes were about the stimulation and enjoyment of being in a research group. Two were

188 • Connecting and Cooperating

about support from and connections with other academics. The final theme was an instrumental one, about doing research and getting desired outcomes. These themes remind us that examining network ties might reflect the choices that actors make, taking disciplinary practices and funding incentives into account, but may not, on its own, provide information on what they value these ties for.

Table 6.3 Benefits of belonging to research groups

Curiosity (22) Intellectual stimulation Keep up to date Sharing ideas Strengthen focus	**Support (21)** Encouragement Intellectual support Learning from senior colleagues Mentoring Constructive criticism/feedback Reduces isolation
Fun (5) Enjoyable Interesting Provides energy Job satisfaction	**Network (14)** Multidisciplinarity Cross-fertilisation Extends contacts/links Dialogue Greater contribution by working together
Instrumental (23) Spreads the workload Can manage larger studies Ensures investing time and energy wisely Joint writing benefits More publications More chance of getting grants Stronger research outcomes Career benefits Raises profile of discipline	

Conclusions

This chapter explored research networks as social capital-producing sites that have the potential to generate knowledge. National research policy that encourages academics to collaborate is a policy intervention that aims to increase the resources that academics can access through links to other academics. Publications data, one marker of the outputs of collaboration, illustrates the range of disciplinary practices operating in different parts of the academy, particularly in terms of whether solo or co-authorship is more common, and thus the differential impact of disciplinary practices on publication. It also provides a picture of the starting point from which different academics begin when they are encouraged by policy interventions to form collaborations.

Proximity is a key organising principle of networks, and various forms of proximity were investigated in this study. For the humanities and social science academics interviewed, the propensity was to form research networks with those from other universities, but from the same discipline and of the same gender. Though the majority of ties were personally close, many were not. The reasons for linking to other academics varied from intellectual curiosity and enjoyment to support and encouragement, and to getting research done and producing outputs.

These analyses have implications for what public policy can and should do to encourage collaboration. Using policy to increase research networks by funding collaboration may build social capital for those involved, but it might also stifle innovation and knowledge creation rather than encourage it if academics' reasons for doing it are purely instrumental. Stimulating collaboration through funding is a means to overcome a lack of social capital for some academics, particularly early career researchers, who lack research connections. Without these networks and the resources they generate, academics can flounder due to a lack of peer support and interaction. Increasing collaboration through policy interventions should have positive effects on knowledge generation, as long as the needs of different disciplines are recognised. Given the very different practices across the academy, different types of collaborative structures will be appropriate in different situations. There is more than one right way to build collaborations and social capital, and generate the research outcomes desired, and only a sophisticated understanding of disciplinary differences will result in increased social capital and more knowledge generation.

7 Conclusion

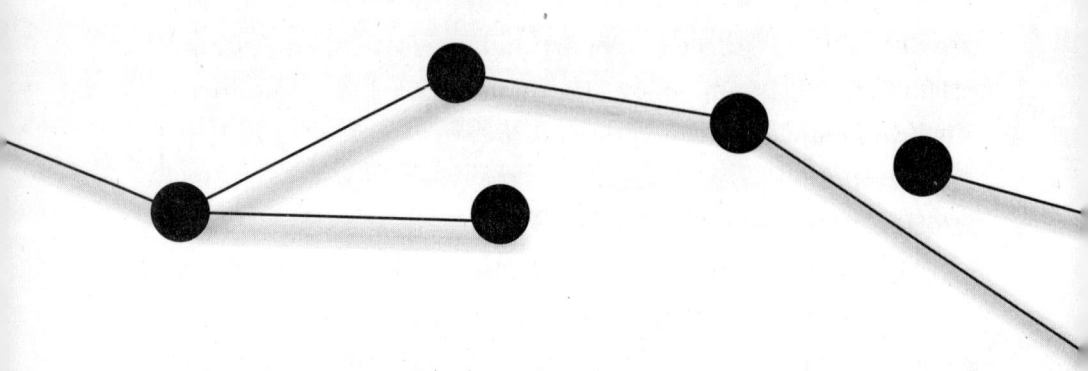

Although the idea of social capital has been around for a long time, it is only in the last decade that it has generated substantial popular interest and public policy attention. Robert Putnam's thesis that civil society has declined over the last half century resonated with the anxiety from the left of politics about the dominance of economic concerns and the lack of interest in the social (typified by Margaret Thatcher's famous 'there's no such thing as society' statement). On the right, social capital ideas became the reason to argue that the state should stop crowding out civil society, and leave individuals to join clubs and talk to their neighbours, which would build this newly valued form of capital. The vagueness of the concept and its normatively positive overtones have ensured that everyone has agreed that it is something we need.

Underpinning this vagueness are serious definitional

differences. In *Bowling Alone*, social capital is defined as: 'social networks and the norms of reciprocity and trustworthiness that arise from them' (Putnam 2000: 19). This is the launching pad from which Putnam sets out to demonstrate the collapse of American community. An economist's definition of it as when 'people cooperate more than they "should" according to standard assumptions of individual rationality' (Paldam 2000: 629) is at the extreme end of rational choice versions, where social capital is seen as something that should only be encouraged when markets and states fail. Neither the claim from Putnam (2006) that 'reaching out to a neighbour or connecting with a long-lost pal – even having a picnic or two – could just save your life' nor Ron Burt's claim that 'the advantage created by a person's location in a structure of relationships is known as social capital' (2005: 4), end up providing the foundation that is needed. There have been some serious social network-based attempts to understand social capital as something that inheres in social relations, something that is in some cases deliberately used to achieve certain outcomes, as per Nan Lin's definition, in which social capital is 'the resources embedded in social networks accessed and used by actors for actions' (2001: 25). This overly rational view is improved by a recognition that social capital can also be something that is unconsciously accessed in the form of emotional support.

Social capital has sparked much interest from academics and been taken up by state institutions in Australia, including the Productivity Commission, the Australian Bureau of Statistics, and some government departments. Governments have deliberately applied social capital ideas to a range of policy areas in the

UK and other European nations, in attempts to combat social exclusion through neighbourhood renewal programs, via policies that have tried to change the mix of housing, investments in transport and public space, and endeavours to reduce health inequalities. International institutions such as the World Bank and the Organization for Economic Cooperation and Development have spent time and energy discussing it and measuring it across nations. This broad acceptance into public discussions, plus increasingly frequent mentions in public policy circles, has not resulted in the meaning of 'social capital' becoming less vague, complicated or strongly contested.

Policy over the last decade has claimed much about the benefits of social capital. Most often the focus has been on its potential for improving citizen engagement, building community, and increasing social inclusion. This focus is welcome. But the means by which government might facilitate the positive aspects of social capital and these valued outcomes are by no means clear. Can the shift to new models of coordination actually increase cooperation between organisations and individuals? If it does, can these new approaches successfully tackle disadvantage of various kinds? Policy-making attempts to increase knowledge generation through collaboration are also social capital-building endeavours, although they are less often explicitly regarded as such. Can efforts to improve connections help in the generation of new knowledge?

A different but important matter in relation to connecting social capital with public policy is how it affects the policy process. What can putting policy making under the microscope, with the use of social capital as a framework, tell us about how individuals and groups wield power and get policy changed? It is extremely rare to find any consideration of this in either the public policy or the social capital literature.

In the first chapter of this book I provided an overview of the critiques of Putnam's work on social capital, and a description of the work of James Coleman and Pierre Bourdieu, before working through Lin's (less well-known) theory in some detail. Social capital, as it appears in *Bowling Alone*, has been described as problematic because of its conflation of individual, organisational and societal levels of analysis, and has been criticised because of Putnam's dubious use of empirical data to demonstrate a decline in civil society, without analysing the changed historical, political, ideological and economic context. An apparent assumption that trust is always an outcome of connections between people, which renders social capital inherently good and always associated with the common good, exacerbated the definitional problems. Finally, his seeming willingness to see difference as a bad thing (since social unity is the goal), and his indifference to the role of governments in building social capital, beyond encouraging the growth of voluntary associations (see Putnam & Feldstein 2003), have spurred many tracts critical of his view of social capital.

Bourdieu argues that all forms of capital (economic, cultural and social) are linked and that the accumulation of social capital, like other forms of capital, is an unequal process. His definition allows for a strongly networked version of social capital at the individual level, which assumes neither that social capital accumulation is related to trust and shared norms, nor that its benefits are equally distributed across society. Coleman's work also rests on a strong network basis, seeing social capital as something that inheres in relations and provides access to resources; however, he did not share Bourdieu's interest in examining which societal groups the resources accumulated to. Lin's focus on action as an important component of social capital is a useful addition to these earlier works. While he sits squarely in the camp of rational choice, he makes some important conceptual points about the level of analysis (individual), and the levels at which social capital accumulates (various). He also makes explicit use of social network concepts beyond density and closure (as per Bourdieu, Coleman and Putnam), such as weak ties, brokerage and heterophily (as per Burt and Granovetter), and distinguishes between expressive and instrumental action in relation to bonding and reaching out to access different resources.

In the second chapter of this book, I built a framework that incorporates a set of parameters for social capital that can be valuable in understanding public policy and directing policy interventions. This framework is divided into three central concerns of social capital theories. These relate to levels of social capital, forms and types of ties, and the accumulation and use of social capital. In regard to levels, I suggested that social capital is best conceived of at the individual level, that it is about individuals in networks, that its benefits can accrue to individuals and groups, that it is a multi-level concept and that there are interactions between the levels. In relation to forms and types of ties, I argued that the different forms of social capital (bonding, bridging and linking) are important, that it is based both on instrumental and expressive ties, that ties have meaning in and of themselves and that there are interactions between different forms of social capital. In relation to the accumulation and use of social capital, I argued for the importance of acknowledging that it takes time to accumulate, that it is about action as well as structure, that the causes and consequences of social capital are separate but interlinked, that there are interactions between both levels and forms of social capital, and that its consequences are neither inherently positive nor inherently negative.

In summary, the framework outlined in Chapter 2 is explicitly focused on individual actors and the connections between them. That is, it rests on social networks. Starting from a rational choice basis that sees social capital as access to resources provided through networks, resources that actors use for actions, I argue that a definition of 'social capital' based on social network concepts is the most accurate and the most productive.

Following this parameter setting, and given the concentration on networks, I briefly reviewed networks and complexity theory to help understand how social capital can be useful for analysing the public policy process, and for directing it so that it increases social capital. Both networks as a concept and network analysis as a means for measuring interconnectedness are important for understanding and examining social capital. The literature on interorganisational networks, policy networks and network governance was used to highlight networks at the meso and macro levels of analysis, most often for metaphorical purposes. Social network analysis operates at the micro level of analysis and provides an opportunity to gain greater empirical purchase on relationships between actors. Some of the best literature on social capital rests on social network concepts and analytical techniques.

Complexity theory also offers some useful ways of thinking about richly connected worlds, and getting beyond seeing the circularity in social capital as a problem. Social capital sits comfortably in such systems, where interconnectedness is central and linearity does not apply. There are some clear benefits in using social capital theory to analyse the policy process, as it explicitly recognises this interconnectedness. There are also benefits to be gained from using networks and complexity theory to guide policy making which needs to cross boundaries (portfolio, sectoral and levels of government), as this is the only approach likely to work in addressing contemporary social problems. Targeted interventions that attempt to join things up within specific contexts and particular locations have increased over the last decade and many of them represent attempts to build social capital.

Schuller, Baron and Field (2000) claim that policy interventions to increase social capital need to devolve power down to local levels, to build links across policy sectors, and to disperse decision making from governments to community organisations. This top-down prescription is at odds with bottom-up developments, but the crux of the matter for policy is whether it is operating on the causes or the consequences of a lack of social capital (Daly & Silver 2008). Short-term benefits might accrue to local communities from policy interventions that aim to enhance connections and cooperation, but long-term benefits will accrue only through a combination of these alongside larger investments that operate at the societal level. Social capital, like any other policy intervention, will not be the panacea that fixes all of society's problems, but it seems that it can make some things better.

An examination of what has been claimed about the link between policy and social capital generation led into a discussion of the methodological challenges faced in turning social capital into something that can be sensibly and meaningfully measured and used in public policy. It is no simple matter to describe the impacts of policies on social ties. If social capital is fundamentally a relational concept, its measurement must be relational too. Social network analysis offers a set of concepts and techniques that can deal with this, but this requires a rethink of the scope of and methods used for such evaluations. It also requires academics (outside the small but growing group of dedicated social network analysts), policy makers, and people in general to become familiar with a new set of concepts and language about nodes, ties and network structures and sub-structures.

In the four chapters that provide illustrative cases, I worked through two examples that demonstrated that the social capital framework of this book can be useful in understanding the policy process, and two examples that examined policy making that aims to increase social capital. In the first of the cases on understanding the policy process, which dealt with influence and agenda setting in policy, the benefits of being well connected personally and within the important positional subgroups were clear: the well connected have a greater ability to set the policy agenda. In the second, which assessed the impact of networks on innovation within governments, it was apparent that those who are innovators are also very central in informal communication networks and that their position in these networks may be more important than their formal role and hierarchical position. Applying this social capital framework to examining public policy can provide insights into the relational aspects of policy making that are obscured by the more common analyses of the policy process, which cast it as a product of institutions and interests and (sometimes) ideas.

If the goal of public policy is to build social capital, what kind of policy interventions should be pursued? Where are the boundaries of what government should do, and what should be left to others? Since government cannot help but have an impact on social relations, even when it has no intention of doing so, the first principle should be that government should try to avoid doing harm. Beyond this, it seems that investments in societal-level programs along with targeted interventions that are sensitive to context will be needed for long-term improvements. It is abundantly clear that little is known about how policy impacts on the networks that are valuable for people in specific situations. There are some excellent social network-based studies that reveal what kinds of networks help people in certain situations, and these provide hope that much more can be done on this front. But much more is unknown than is known. Associated with this is the risk for policy makers of implementing initiatives that cannot be evaluated clearly. Without persuasive evidence that such interventions work, the political risks of introducing policies that aim to build social capital (not to mention the societal risks) are high.

Place-based policies have been one of the most common in the range of initiatives that rest on social capital concepts. The first illustrative case in this book was on place-based partnerships of two different kinds. The partnerships that aimed to increase service coordination in primary healthcare demonstrated that social capital can be built between agencies when an outside broker is brought in and time is spent on joining agencies up to deal with common problems at the local level. It also showed that removing that social capital builder (the broker) is likely to result in the goodwill being lost. The lesson for government is that if service coordination of a fragmented system is the goal (along with the supposed improved health outcomes that will follow from it in time), an ongoing commitment to providing the glue that holds it together is likely to be required. The second type of partnership, which aimed to build communities in areas of disadvantage, likewise worked well in creating relationships. However, this was a case where government could probably provide start-up funds and then move out, leaving it to the partnership to carry on the work of building social capital. Both of these partnership types pointed to the need for government to act as facilitator rather than director of the initiatives at the local level. Neither of these examples was capable of overcoming disadvantage without the higher level interventions that signal, as Simon Szreter (2002) pointed out, that the government provides systems and services to help when help is needed. A focus on the local level, which is widely seen as the appropriate level of intervention for social capital initiatives that tackle disadvantage, should not detract from this important larger context, which establishes the extent to which people feel connected into society and valued as citizens.

The second case, focused on knowledge generation, was a very different type of policy intervention, even though it was based on setting up linkages between individuals and their organisations and assumed that the benefits in terms of new knowledge arising from collaboration would be greater than those that individual researchers and universities could achieve alone. Those targeted were generally rather economically privileged, not disadvantaged, and the outcomes desired related to improving knowledge generation by elites, not to fixing service disconnects or improving individual connections in certain localities. This case highlighted the fact that some have few incentives to build social capital. Some readily worked with others to generate knowledge and some did not. This was related more to traditional disciplinary practices than to what governments might do to encourage them to collaborate. The networks that helped support knowledge generation were also more discussion based in some parts of the academy than in others. Targeting funds at collaboration activities without a nuanced understanding of these differences could lead to supporting those who already work in this way. At best, it would be irrelevant for those whose work does not fit well with these more instrumental collaborations. At worst, it would force some people into networks that would be either a waste of time or actually destructive of social capital.

This book sheds light on how social capital can be used to scrutinise the policy-making process. Conceiving of social capital as the access that individuals have, through their networks, to embedded resources, and then observing the varying levels of resources they have and how they use them to achieve desired outcomes, is a novel means of studying the policy process. It demonstrates that the old adage – it is not only what you know, but who you know – is surely true. It also proves that your location, in network terms, can be more important than other factors in determining your ability to make policy.

Making public policy that increases social capital is high on the agenda of modern governments. It is clear that doing so requires a serious empirical analysis of who will benefit in what circumstances, and part of this involves having a solid grip on what kinds of networks need to be built and what kinds of ideal patterns of relationships (network structures and substructures) are best for addressing particular problems. Social network analysis provides concepts and techniques for understanding what these interventions look like, and for evaluating the impacts of policies that aim to build social capital. These less than familiar concepts and techniques require a rethink of methodologies, but alongside assessments of the achievements and outcomes of specific policy interventions, they promise much greater clarity in being able to say what works, for whom, and in what circumstances.

Some ground has been gained here, but much work remains to be done. Some promising answers emerge from this book in response to the question: what should governments do to build social capital? Choosing an appropriate framework for analysing social capital and its link to public policy is a good start. Focusing on the causes and consequences of disadvantage, as well as the need for government to devolve power to the local level, to engage in linking across policy sectors and to disperse decision making to communities, leads to policy prescriptions that can produce long-term change by combining large-scale investments with local interventions. Improving knowledge generation through collaboration also requires devolution and dispersion (in regard to disciplinary differences) so that the benefits are not confined to only some researchers. Sophisticated methodologies that are premised on relational data and so are able to treat networks seriously in evaluations should improve the information that guides the policy process. All of these together suggest a better analysis of the policy process, as well as policy interventions that should generate more connecting and cooperating.

Notes

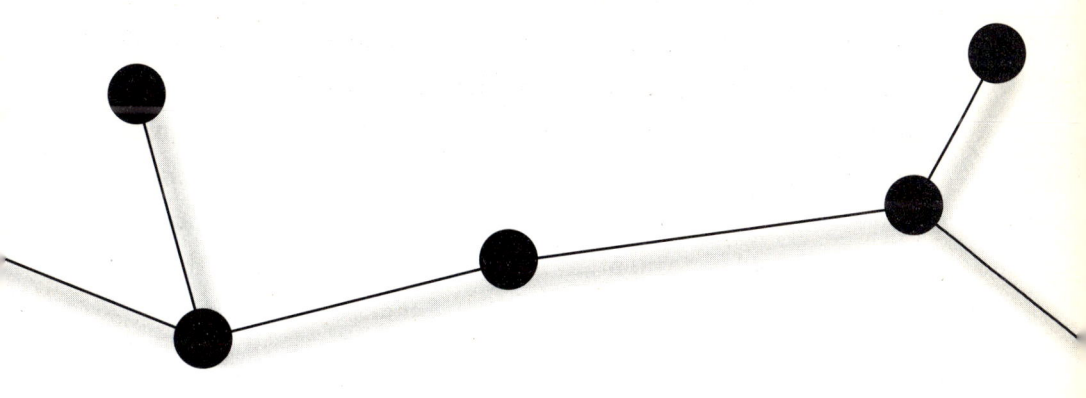

Chapter 3

1. While each new set of nominations adds new names, after five steps out from the starting point, the number of new names being added began to drop. The progression was from 1 person in the first round, to 16 in the second round, 31 in the third round, 65 in the fourth round, 64 in the fifth round, and then 41 in the sixth round.
2. While the response rate is not high, at 54 per cent, there were no major discrepancies between nominees and respondents based on location, discipline and gender, as outlined in the previous section.
3. There were two medicals schools in Victoria at the time of this study – one at the University of Melbourne and one at Monash University. La Trobe University had a large faculty of health sciences, which did not include medicine at this time.
4. 'Public health' does not mean the publicly funded healthcare system. It is a term used to encompass disease prevention and health promotion for populations. It is very multidisciplinary, but all the people in this block had medical qualifications. This label does not indicate that everyone in this group is in the public health medicine faculty of the Royal Australasian College of Physicians.
5. The information from the blockmodel combined with the number of times individuals had been nominated was used to draw up a list of potential interviewees. On the basis of the number of nominations received and coverage of 7 of the 8 blocks (with the Defined areas block excluded), 21 people were selected for interviews. One person declined to be interviewed.
6. VicHealth is the Victorian Health Promotion Foundation – a statutory authority funded by the state government but separate from the state health bureaucracy.

7   These total 107 mentions of issues – so on average, interviewees discussed about 5 issues each. Issues were identified both during the interviews and recorded as notes, and through a systematic analysis of the transcripts of each of the 20 interviews. The transcripts of the interviews were thematically coded and then re-examined and, in some cases, re-coded.

Chapter 4

1   Using volunteers skews the sample towards those more interested in the topic of innovation. This bias is not important for my purposes here, but does limit how far the findings can be generalised to all governments.
2   The actual questions were: 'Looking back over the last 6 months, who are the people you went to most when you wanted to *get advice* on a work-related issue (including career, job or program advice)?' and 'Over the last 6 months, who did you go to most when you wanted to get *strategic information* about something in the Government/organisation (including background information not yet available in reports etc)?' For the advice question, respondents could nominate any five individuals they chose. For the strategic information question nominations were limited to five people from within their own organisation.
3   Normalisation makes them comparable across networks (governments) of different sizes (Scott 2000). This is important, given the variation in size of the governments.
4   While nomination-based methods for locating key actors have attracted criticism for being highly subjective, when dealing with small and medium-sized groups who work in close proximity to one another, it is reasonable to expect that they will be well informed about one another's reputation for work-related performance.
5   In total, 464 nominations were received across the four local governments. Only politicians and bureaucrats were nominated, with not a single nomination directed to actors outside.

Chapter 5

1   These two partnerships were chosen because DHS saw them as likely to be successful, based on their initial community health plans. They do not necessarily reflect all PCPs.
2   In the first year, interviews were conducted face to face, and averaged around one hour to complete. In the second and third years, interviews were conducted by telephone, and took between 30 and 45 minutes. All interviews were recorded and transcribed. See Lewis, Baeza and Alexander (2008) for further details.
3   The actual questions used were: 'Looking back over the last 6 months, who are the people you had the most contact with *in order to do your work*?' and 'Over the last 6 months, who did you go to most when you wanted to get *strategic information about something in the PCP*?'.
4   The interviews were recorded and transcribed. For Campaspe, the number of people interviewed was 18, 20 and 20 in each of the three years of the study, and for Westbay, 19 people were interviewed in each year.
5   This was out of an identified sample of 139 (86 per cent response rate). Four people refused to participate, and 10 declined because they were recently appointed and felt they could not comment. Five could not be contacted, and one undertook the interview but declined to list their contacts. See Pope and Lewis (2008) for further details.

Bibliography

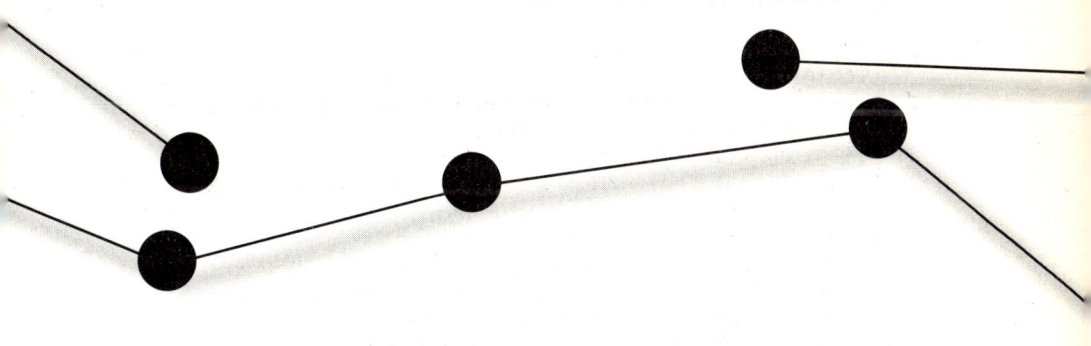

6, P (2004) Can government influence our friendships? The range and limits of tools for trying to shape solidarities. In Chris Phillipson, Graham Allan & David HJ Morgan (eds) *Social Networks and Social Exclusion: Sociological and Policy Perspectives*, Ashgate Publishing, Aldershot: 180–204.

Adam, F & Roncevic, B (2003) Social capital: Recent debates and research trends, *Social Science Information*, 42(2): 155–83.

Agranoff, R (2007) *Managing within networks: Adding value to public organizations*, Georgetown University Press, Washington.

Agranoff, R & McGuire, M (2001) After the network is formed: Process, power and performance. In Myrna P Mandell (ed.) *Getting Results through Collaboration: Networks and network structures for public policy and management*, Quorum Books, Westport CT.

Akkerman, T, Hajer, M & Grin, J (2004) The interactive state: Democratisation from above?, *Political Studies* 52: 82–95.

Alford, J & Considine, M (1994) Public sector employment contracts. In John Alford and Deirdre O'Neill (eds) *The Contract State: Public management and the Kennett Government*, Deakin University Press, Geelong.

Alford, R (1975) *Health Care Politics: Ideological and interest group barriers to reform*, The University of Chicago Press, Chicago.

Arneil, B (2006) *Diverse Communities: The problem with social capital*, Cambridge University Press, Cambridge.

Arora, S, Davies, A & Thompson, S (2000) Developing health improvement programmes: Challenges for a new millennium, *Journal of Interprofessional Care*, 14(1): 9–18.

Audit Commission (1998) *A Fruitful Partnership: Effective partnership working*, Audit Commission, London.

Australian Bureau of Statistics (ABS) (2004) *Measuring Social Capital: An Australian framework and indicators*, Commonwealth of Australia, Canberra.

Australian Institute for Primary Care (July 2002) *Evaluation of the Primary Care Partnership Strategy: Baseline report*, La Trobe University, Melbourne.

—— (2003) *An Evaluation of the Primary Care Partnership Strategy: Final report*, La Trobe University, Melbourne.

Barabási, AL (2002) *Linked: The new science of networks*, Perseus, Cambridge, MA.

Baron, S, Field, J & Schuller, T (eds) (2000) *Social Capital: Critical perspectives*, Oxford University Press, New York.

Barzeley, M & Gallego, R (2006) From 'New Institutionalism' to 'Institutional Processualism': Advancing knowledge about public management policy change, *Governance*, 19(4): 531–57.

Bauld, L, Judge, K, Barnes, M, Benzeval, M, Mackenzie, M & Sullivan, H (2005) Promoting social change: The experience of Health Action Zones in England, *Journal of Social Policy*, 34: 427–45.

Beauvais, C & Jenson, J (2002) Social Cohesion: Updating the state of the research, CPRN Discussion Paper No. F|22, Canadian Policy Research Networks Inc., Ottawa.

Bebbington, A, Guggenheim, S, Olsen, E & Woolcock, M (2004) Exploring social capital debates at the World Bank, *The Journal of Development Studies*, 40(5): 33–64.

Benington, J (2001) Partnerships as networked governance? Legitimation, innovation, problem solving and co-ordination. In Mike Geddes and John Benington (eds) *Local Partnerships and Social Exclusion in the European Union*, Routledge, London.

Benson, JK (1982) A framework for policy analysis. In David Rogers and David A Whetten (eds) *Interorganizational Coordination: Theory, research, and implementation*, Iowa State University Press, Ames IO: 137–76.

Bolland, J & Wilson, J (1994) Three faces of integrative coordination: A model of interorganizational relations in community-based health and human services, *Health Services Research*, 29(3): 341–66.

Borgatti, S, Everett, M & Freeman, L (2002) *UCINET 6.0*, Analytic Technologies, Natick MA.

Borins, S (2000) Loose cannons and rule breakers, or enterprising leaders? Some evidence about innovative public managers, *Public Administration Review*, 60(6): 498–507.

Bourdieu, P (1986) The forms of capital. In John G Richardson (ed.) *Handbook of Theory and Research for the Sociology of Education*, Greenwood Press, New York: 241–58.

—— (1989) Social space and symbolic power, *Sociological Theory*, 7(1): 14–25.

Bourdieu, P & Passeron, JC (1977) *Reproduction in Education, Society and Culture*, Sage, London.

Brady, D (1982) Congressional party realignment and transformation of the political agenda, *American Journal of Political Science*, 26: 333–60.

Breiger, RL (1976) Career attributes and network structure: A blockmodel study of a biomedical research speciality, *American Sociological Review*, 41(1): 117–35.

Bryson, L & Mowbray, M (2005) More spray on solution: Community, social capital and evidence based policy, *The Australian Journal of Social Issues*, 40(1): 91–106.

Burt, RS (1984) Network items and the General Social Survey, *Social Networks*, 6(4): 293–339.
—— (1992) *Structural Holes: The social structure of competition*, Harvard University Press, Cambridge MA.
—— (2005) *Brokerage and Closure: An introduction to social capital*, Cambridge University Press, Cambridge.
Byrne, D (1998) *Complexity Theory and the Social Sciences*, Routledge, London.
Cabinet Office (1998) *Modernising Government*, HMSO, London.
Canadian Policy Research Initiative (2003a) *Social Capital: Building on a network-based approach*, Draft Discussion Paper, Policy Research Initiative, Government of Canada.
—— (2003b) *Social Capital as a Public Policy Tool: Social capital workshop June 2003 (Concepts, measurement and policy implications)*, report of findings, Policy Research Initiative, Government of Canada.
Child, J & Faulkner, D (1998) *Strategies of Cooperation: Managing alliances, networks, and joint ventures*, Oxford University Press, Oxford.
Cilliers, P (1998) *Complexity and Postmodernism*, Routledge, London.
Cobb, RW & Elder, CD (1971) The politics of agenda building: An alternative perspective for modern democratic theory, *Journal of Politics*, 33: 892–915.
Coleman, JS (1988) Social capital in the creation of human capital, *The American Journal of Sociology*, 94 (Supplement: Organizations and Institutions: Sociological and Economic Approaches to the Analysis of Social Structure): S95–S120.
—— (1994) *Foundations of Social Theory*, Belknap Press, Cambridge MA.
Coleman, JS, Katz, E & Menzel, H (1966) *Medical Innovation: A diffusion study*, Bobbs Merrill, New York.
Considine, M & Lewis, JM (1999) Governance at ground level: The frontline bureaucrat in the age of markets and networks, *Public Administration Review*, 59(6): 467–80.
—— (2003) Bureaucracy, network or enterprise? Comparing models of governance in Australia, Britain, the Netherlands, and New Zealand, *Public Administration Review* 63(2): 131–40.
—— (2005) Mapping the normative underpinnings of local governance. In Paul Smyth, Tim Reddel & Andrew Jones (eds) *Community and Local Governance in Australia*, UNSW Press, Sydney: 205–25.
—— (2007) Innovation and innovators inside government from institutions to networks, *Governance* 20(4): 581–607.
Considine, M, Lewis, JM & Alexander, D (2008) Governance, networks and civil society: How local governments connect to local organisations and groups. In Jo Barraket (ed.) *Strategic issues in the not-for-profit sector*, UNSW Press, Sydney: 74–102.
—— (2009) *Networks, Innovation and Public Policy: Politicians, bureaucrats and the pathways to change inside government*, Palgrave Macmillan, Houndmills.
Conway, S (1995) Informal boundary-spanning communication in the innovation process, *Technology Analysis and Strategic Management*, 7(3): 327–42.
Coveney, P & Highfield, R (1995) *Frontiers of Complexity: The search for order in a chaotic world*, Faber & Faber, London.
Cox, E (2000). Creating a more civil society: Community level indicators of social capital, *Just Policy*, 19(20): 100–07.
Damanpour, F (1991) Organisational Innovation: A meta-analysis of effects of

determinants and moderators, *Academy of Management Journal*, 34(3): 555–90.
Daly, M & Silver, H (2008) Social exclusion and social capital: A comparison and critique, *Theory and Society*, 37: 537–66.
Diani, M (2003) Introduction: Social movements, contentious actions, and social networks: from metaphor to substance. In Mario Diani and Doug McAdam (eds) *Social Movements and Networks: Relational approaches to collective action*, Oxford University Press, Oxford.
Degenne, A & Forse, M (1999) *Introducing Social Networks*, Sage, London.
Department of Human Services (DHS) (1998) *A Stronger Primary Health and Community Support System: Policy Directions*, State of Victoria, Melbourne.
—— (2000) *Primary Care Partnerships: Going forward*, State of Victoria, Melbourne.
Department of Planning and Community Development (DPCD) (2007) *Strengthening Local Communities: Integrated local area planning in growth suburbs: The evaluation of the Caroline Springs Partnership*, Department of Planning and Community Development, Melbourne. Available at: http://www.dvc.vic.gov.au/web14/dvc/dvcmain.nsf/headingpagesdisplay/research+and+publicationsresearch+and+other+information [last accessed 8 February 2008].
Dodgson, M & Bessant, J (1996) *Effective Innovation Policy: A new approach*, International Thomson Business Press, London.
Drucker, P (1985) *Innovation and Entrepreneurship*, Heinemann, London.
Durlauf, S & Fafchamps, M (2004) *Social Capital*, CSAE WPS/2004–14, Oxford.
Edwards, B & Foley, MW (1998) Civil society and social capital beyond Putnam, *American Behavioural Scientist*, 124(1): 124–39.
Emery, F, & Trist, E (1965) The causal texture of organizational environments, *Human Relations*, 18: 21–32.
Ferlie, E & McGivern, G (2003) *Relationships Between Health Care Organisations*, NCCSDO, London.
Field, J (2003) *Social Capital*, Routledge, New York.
Fine, B (1999) A question of economics: Is it colonizing the social sciences?, *Economy and Society*, 28(3): 403–25.
Finsveen, E & Oorschot, WV (2008) Access to resources in networks: A theoretical and empirical critique of networks as a proxy for social capital, *Acta Sociologica*, 51(4): 293–307.
Freeman, C (1991) Networks of innovators: A synthesis of research issues, *Research Policy*, 20(5): 499–514.
Friedkin, N (1998) *A Structural Theory of Social Influence*, Cambridge University Press, New York.
Fuller, S (2000) *The Governance of Science: Ideology and the future of the open society*, Open University Press, Buckingham.
Geddes, M & Benington, J (eds) (2001) *Local Partnerships and Social Exclusion in the European Union*, Routledge, London.
Giddens, A (1984) *The Constitution of Society: Outline of the theory of structuration*, Polity Press, Cambridge.
Glendinning, C, Coleman, A, Shipman, C & Malbon, G (2001) Progress in partnerships, *BMJ*, 323: 28–30.
Granovetter, M (1973) The strength of weak ties, *American Journal of Sociology*, 78(6): 1360–80.
Haas, P (1992) Introduction: Epistemic communities and international policy coordination, *International Organization*, 46(1): 1–35.

Hage, J & Alter, C (1997) A typology of inter-organizational relationships and networks. In J Rogers Hollingsworth and Robert Boyer (eds) *Contemporary Capitalism*, Cambridge University Press, Cambridge: 94–126.

Halpern, D (2005) *Social Capital*, Polity Press, Cambridge.

Hardy, B, Hudson, B & Waddington, E (2003) *Assessing Strategic Partnership: The partnership assessment tool*, Office of the Deputy Prime Minister, London.

Hawley, W, & Svara, J (1972) *The Study of Community Power: A bibliographic review*, American Bibliographic Center-Clio Press, Santa Barbara, CA.

Hay, C (2002) *Political Analysis: A critical introduction*, Palgrave, Houndmills.

Hayden, C & Benington, J (2000) Multi-level networked governance – Reflections from the better government for older people programme, *Public Money and Management*, 20(2): 27–34.

Healy, T (2004) Social capital: Old hat or new insight?, *Irish Journal of Sociology*, 13(1): 5–28.

Horton, S (2006) Social capital, government policy and public value: Implications for archive delivery, Aslib Proceedings, *New Information Perspectives*, 58(6): 502–12.

Howe, B & Cleary, R (2001) *Community Building: Policy issues and strategies for the Victorian Government*, Department of Premier and Cabinet, Melbourne.

Hudson, B & Hardy, B (2001) Localization and partnership in the 'New National Health Service': England and Scotland compared, *Public Administration*, 79(2): 315–35.

Huxham, C & Vangen, S (2005) *Managing to Collaborate: The theory and practice of collaborative advantage*, Routledge, London.

Ibarra, H (1992) Homophily and differential returns: Sex differences in network structure and access in an advertising firm, *Administrative Science Quarterly*, 37(3): 422–47.

Ibarra, H (1997) Paving an alternative route: Gender differences in managerial networks, *Social Psychology Quarterly*, 60(1): 91–102.

Ingram, P and Roberts, PW (2000) Friendship among competitors in the Sydney hotel industry, *American Journal of Sociology*, 106(2): 387–423.

International Network for Social Network Analysis website <www.insna.org>.

Jessop, B (2001) Institutional (re)turns and the strategic-relational approach, *Environment and Planning A*, 33(7): 1213–35.

Johnson, D, Headey, B & Jensen, B (2003) *Communities, social capital and public policy: Literature review*, Melbourne Institute of Applied Economies and Social Research, Melbourne.

Johnson, C & Osborne, SP (2003) Local strategic partnerships, neighbourhood renewal, and the limits of co-governance, *Public Money and Management*, 23(3): 147–54.

Jones, O, Conway, S & Steward, F (1998) Introduction: Social interaction and innovation networks, *International Journal of Innovation Management* (Special Issue) 2(2): 123–36.

Jones, O & Beckinsale, M (1999) *Analysing the Innovation Process: Networks, micropolitics and structural change*, Research Paper 9919, Aston Business School, Aston University, Birmingham.

Kadushin, C (1968) Power, influence and social circles: A new methodology for studying opinion-makers, *American Sociological Review*, 33: 685–99.

—— (2004) Too much investment in social capital?, *Social Networks*, 26(1): 75–90.

Kanter, R (1985) *The Change Makers*, Unwin, London.
Keast, R, Mandell, MP, Brown, K & Woolcock, G (2004) Network structures: Working differently and changing expectations, *Public Administration Review*, 64(3): 363–71.
Kickert, W, Klijn, EH & Koppenjan, J (eds) (1997) *Managing Complex Networks: Strategies for the public sector*, Sage, London.
Kingdon, JW (1995). *Agendas, alternatives, and public policies* (2nd edn), HarperCollins, New York.
Kjaer, AM (2004) *Governance*, Polity, Cambridge.
Klijn, EH & Koppenjan, JFM (2004) *Managing Uncertainties in Networks: A network approach to problem solving and decision-making*, Routledge, London.
Klijn, EH & Skelcher, C (2007) Democracy and Governance Networks: Compatible or not?, *Public Administration*, 85(3): 587–608.
Knoke, D (1990) *Political Networks: The structural perspective*, Cambridge, New York.
—— (2001) *Changing Organizations: Business networks in the new political economy*, Westview Press, Boulder CO.
Kooiman, J (ed.) (1993) *Modern Governance: New government–society interactions*, Sage, London.
—— (2003) *Governing as Governance*, Sage, London.
Krackhardt, D (1992) The Strength of Strong Ties: The importance of philos in organizations. In Nitin Nohria & Robert G Eccles (eds) *Networks and Organizations: Structure, form, and action*, Harvard Business School Press, Boston: 216–39.
Laumann, E & Knoke, D (1987) *The Organizational State: Social choice in national policy domains*, University of Wisconsin Press, Madison WI.
Le Grand, J & Barlett, W (1993) *Quasi-markets and Social Policy*, Macmillan, London.
Lewis, JM (1999) The durability of ideas in health policy making. In Dietmar Braun & Andreas E Busch (eds) *Public Policy and Political Ideas*, Edward Elgar, Cheltenham: 152–67.
—— (2004) Partnerships, primary health care and health inequalities: Problems and possibilities, *Australian Journal of Primary Health*, 10(3): 38–45.
—— (2005a) *Health Policy and Politics: Networks, ideas and power*, IP Communications, Melbourne.
—— (2005b) A network approach for researching partnerships in health, *Australia and New Zealand Health Policy* 2: 22.
—— (2006) Being around and knowing the players: Networks of influence in health policy, *Social Science and Medicine*, 62(9): 2125–136.
Lewis, JM, Baeza, JI & Alexander, D (2008) Partnerships in primary care: Network structures, dynamics and sustainability, *Social Science and Medicine*, 67(2): 280–91.
Lewis, JM, & Considine, M (1999) Medicine, economics and agenda setting, *Social Science & Medicine*, 48: 393–405.
Li, Y, Pickles, A & Savage, M (2005) Social capital and social trust in Britain, *European Sociological Review*, 21(2): 109–23.
Lin, N (1982) Social resources and instrumental action. In Peter V Marsden and Nan Lin (eds) *Social Structure and Network Analysis*, Sage, Beverley Hills CA: 131–45.

—— (2001) *Social Capital: A theory of social structure and action*, Cambridge University Press, New York.
Lin, N, Cook, KS & Burt, RS (2001) *Social Capital: Theory and research*, Aldine de Gruyter, New York.
Lin, N & Dumin, M (1986) Access to occupations through social ties, *Social Networks*, 8: 365–85.
Lin, N & Erickson, BH (2008) Theory, measurement, and the research enterprise on social capital. In Nan Lin and Bonnie H Erickson (eds) *Social Capital: An international research program*, Oxford University Press, Oxford: 1–26.
Little, A (2002) *The Politics of Community: Theory and practice*, Edinburgh University Press, Edinburgh.
Local Government Association (2000) *Partnerships with Health: A survey of local authorities*, Local Government Association, London.
Love, J (1999) *Patterns of Networking in the Innovation Process: A comparative study of the UK, Germany and Ireland*, Research Paper 9913, Aston Business School, Aston University, Birmingham, accessed at <www.abs.aston.ac/UK/>.
Lowndes, V, Nanton, P, McCabe, A & Skelcher, C (1997) Networks, partnerships and urban regeneration, *Local Economy*, 11(4): 333–42.
Lowndes, V & Skelcher, C (1998) The dynamics of multi-organisational partnerships: An analysis of changing modes of governance, *Public Administration*, 76(2): 313–34.
Lundvall, B (ed.) (1992) *National Systems of Innovation*, Pinter, London.
Maloney, WA, Smith, G & Stoker, G (2000) Social capital and associational life. In Stephen Barron, John Field & Tom Schuller, *Social Capital: Critical perspectives*, Oxford University Press, Oxford: 197–211.
Management Advisory Committee (2004) *Connecting Government: Whole of government responses to Australia's priority challenges*, Commonwealth of Australia, Canberra.
Mandell, MP (1999) Community collaborations: Working through network structures, *Policy Studies Review*, 16(1): 42–64.
—— (ed.) (2001) *Getting Results through Collaboration: Networks and network structures for public policy and management*, Quorum Books, Westport CT.
—— (2002–03) Types of collaborations and why the differences really matter, *The Public Manager*, 31(4): 36–40.
Marsden, P (1981) Introducing influence processes into a system of collective decisions, *American Journal of Sociology*, 86: 1203–35.
Marsh, D & Rhodes, R (eds) (1992) *Policy Networks in British Government*, Oxford University Press, Oxford.
Martin, J (2000) Economic and community development through innovative local government, *Sustaining Regions*, 1(1): 1–12.
Maskell, P (2000) Social capital and competitiveness, In Stephen Baron, John Field & Tom Schuller (eds) *Social Capital: Critical perspectives*, Oxford University Press, Oxford: 111–23.
Massey, DS (1996) The age of extremes: Concentrated affluence and poverty in the twenty-first century, *Demography*, 33: 395–412.
McPherson, JM & Smith-Lovin, L (1987) Homophily in voluntary organizations: Status distance and the composition of face-to-face groups, *American Sociological Review*, 52(3): 370–79.
Mintrom, M & Vergari, S (1998) Policy networks and innovation diffusion: The case

of state education reform, *The Journal of Politics*, 60(1): 126–48.

Milward, HB & Provan, KG (1998) Measuring network structure, *Public Administration*, 76(2): 387–407.

Mitchell, S & Shortell, S (2000) The governance and management of effective community health partnerships: A typology for research, policy, and practice, *Milbank Quarterly*, 78(2): 241–89.

Montgomery, J (2005) *Community, Place and Buildings: The role of community facilities in developing community spirit*, Department for Victorian Communities, Melbourne.

Moore, S, Smith, C, Simpson, T & Minke, S (2006) The influence of partnership centrality on organizational perceptions of support: A case study of the AHLN structure, *BMC Health Services Research*, 6: 141.

Mouffe, C (2000) *The Democratic Paradox*, Verso, London and New York.

Mulgan, G & Albury, D (2003) *Innovation in the Public Sector*, The Prime Minster's Strategy Unit, London, accessed at http://www.cabinetoffice.gov.uk/upload/assets/www.cabinetoffice.gov.uk/strategy/pubinov2.pdf.

Munn, P. (2000). Social capital, schools, and education. In Stephen Baron, John Field and Tom Schuller (eds) *Social Capital: Critical perspectives*, Oxford University Press, Oxford: 168–81.

Nash, V (2004) Public policy and social networks: Just how 'socially aware' is the policy-making process? In Chris Phillipson, Graham Allan & David HJ Morgan (eds) *Social Networks and Social Exclusion: Sociological and policy perspectives*, Ashgate Publishing, Aldershot: 219–35.

Newman, J, Raine, J & Skelcher, C (2001) Transforming local government: Innovation and modernization, *Public Money and Management*, 21(2): 61–68.

Onyx, J & Bullen, P (2001) The different faces of social capital in NSW Australia. In Jenny Onyx & Paul Bullen (eds) *Social Capital and Everyday Life*, Routledge, London: 45–58.

Organisation for Economic Cooperation and Development (OECD) (2004) *New Forms of Governance for Economic Development*, OECD, Paris.

O'Toole, L. (1997) Treating networks seriously: Practical and research-based agendas in public administration, *Public Administration Review*, 57(1): 45–51.

Ouchi, W (1980) Markets, bureaucracies, and clans, *Administrative Science Quarterly*, 25(1): 129–41.

Paldam, M (2000) Social capital: One or many? Definition and measurement, *Journal of Economic Surveys*, 14(5): 629–53.

Paterson, L (2000) Civil society and democratic renewal. In Stephen Baron, John Field & Tom Schuller (eds) *Social Capital: Critical perspectives*, Oxford University Press, Oxford: 39–55.

Paxton, P (1999) Is social capital declining in the United States? A multiple indicator assessment, *American Journal of Sociology*, 105(1): 88–127.

Peckham, S, Exworthy, M, Powell, M & Greener, I (2005) *Decentralisation as an Organisational Model for Health Care in England*, NCCSDO, London.

Pierre, J and Peters, BG (2000) *Governance, Politics and the State*, Macmillan, London.

Pope, J (2003) *Social Capital and Social Capital Indicators: A reading list*, Working Paper Series, Public Health Information Development Unit, University of Adelaide.

Pope, J & Lewis, JM (2008) Improving partnership governance: Using a network

approach to evaluate partnerships in Victoria, *Australian Journal of Public Administration*, 67(4): 443–56.
Portes, A (1998) Social capital: Its origins and applications in modern sociology, *Annual Review of Sociology*, 24: 1–24.
—— (2000) The two meanings of social capital, *Sociological Forum*, 15(1): 1–12.
Powell, M & Exworthy, M (2002) Partnerships, quasi-networks and social policy. In Caroline Glendinning, Martin Powell and Kirstein Rummery (eds) *Partnerships, New Labour and the Governance of Welfare*, The Policy Press, Bristol.
Powell, W (1990) Neither market nor hierarchy: Network forms of organization, *Research in Organizational Behaviour*, 12: 295–336.
Pratt, J, Plamping, D & Gordon P (1998) *Partnership fit for Purpose?*, King's Fund, London.
Productivity Commission (2003) *Social Capital: Reviewing the concept and its policy implications*, AusInfo, Canberra.
Provan, KG, Veazie, MA, Staten, LK & Teufel-Shone, NI (2005) The use of network analysis to strengthen community partnerships, *Public Administration Review*, 65(5): 603–13.
Provan, KG, & Milward, HB (1995) A preliminary theory of interorganizational network effectiveness: A comparative study of four community mental health systems, *Administrative Science Quarterly*, 40: 1–33.
—— (2001) Do networks really work? A framework for evaluating public-sector organizational networks, *Public Administration Review*, 61(4): 414–23.
Putnam, R (1995a) Bowling alone: America's declining social capital, *Journal of Democracy*, 6(1): 65.
—— (1995b) Tuning in, tuning out: The strange disappearance of social capital in America, *Political Science and Politics*, 28(4): 664–83.
—— (2000) *Bowling Alone: The collapse and revival of American community*, Simon & Schuster, New York.
—— (2006) You gotta have friends, *Time Magazine*, 25 June.
Putnam, R & Feldstein, L (2003) *Better Together*, Simon & Schuster, New York.
Putnam, R, Leonardi, R & Nanetti, R (1993) *Making Democracy Work: Civic traditions in modern Italy*, Princeton University Press, Princeton NJ.
Rhodes, RAW (1997) *Understanding Governance: Policy networks, governance, reflexivity and accountability*, Open University Press, Buckingham.
—— (2000) The governance narrative, *Public Administration* 78: 345–63.
Rhodes, RAW & Marsh, D (1992) Policy networks in British politics: A critique of existing approaches. In David Marsh and RAW Rhodes, *Policy Networks in British Government*, Oxford University Press, Oxford: 2–27.
Rigby, J & Edler, J (2005) Peering inside research networks: Some observations on the effect of the intensity of collaboration on the variability of research quality, *Research Policy*, 34: 784–94.
Rogers, EM (1995) *Diffusion of Innovations* (4th edn), Free Press, New York.
Rogers, EM & Beal, GM (1958) *Reference Group Influence in the Adoption of Agricultural Technology*, Iowa State University, Ames, IA.
Rogers, EM & Kincaid, DL (1981) *Communication Networks: A new paradigm for research*, Free Press, New York.
Russell, H (1999) Friends in low places: Gender, unemployment and sociability, *Work, Employment & Society*, 13: 205–24.
Sabatier, P (1988) An advocacy coalition framework of policy change and the role of

policy-oriented learning therein, *Policy Sciences*, 21: 129–68.
Sandefur, RL & Laumann, EO (1998) A paradigm for social capital, *Rationality and Society*, 10(4): 481–501.
Sanders, RP (1998) Heroes of the revolution. In Patricia W Ingraham, James R Thompson & Ronald P Sanders (eds) *Transforming Government: Lessons from the reinvention laboratories*, Jossey-Bass, San Francisco.
Scharpf, F (1997) *Games Real Actors Play: Actor-centered institutionalism in policy research*, Westview Press, Boulder CO.
Schuller, T, Baron, S & Field, J (2000) Social capital: A review and critique. In Stephen Baron, John Field and Tom Schuller (eds) *Social Capital: Critical perspectives*, Oxford University Press, Oxford: 1–38.
Scott, J (2000) *Social Network Analysis: A handbook*, Sage, London.
Skelcher, C, McCabe, A, Lowndes, V & Nanton, P (1996) *Community Networks in Urban Regeneration*, The Policy Press, Bristol.
Skok, JE (1995) Policy issue networks and the public policy cycle: A structural-functional framework for public administration, *Public Administration Review*, 55: 325–32.
Slaughter, S & Leslie, L (1997) *Academic Capitalism: Politics, policies and the entrepreneurial university*, Johns Hopkins University Press, Baltimore ML.
Smith, SS & Kulynych, J (2002) It may be social, but why is it capital? The social construction of social capital and the politics of language, *Politics & Society*, 30(1): 149–86.
Smith, M, Mathur, N & Skelcher, C (2006) Corporate governance in a collaborative environment: What happens when government, business and civil society work together?, *Corporate Governance: An international review*, 14(3): 159–71.
Social Exclusion Unit (1999) Policy Action Team Report 9: Community Self-help, Social Exclusion Task Force, London, accessed at: <http://www.cabinetoffice.gov.uk/social_exclusion_task_force/publications.aspx>.
Sørensen, E & Torfing, J (eds) (2007) *Theories of Democratic Network Governance*, Palgrave Macmillan, Houndmills.
State Government of Victoria (2008) *A Fairer Victoria: Strong people, strong communities*, State Government of Victoria, Melbourne.
Straits, BC (2000) Ego's important discussants or significant people: An experiment in varying the wording of personal network name generators, *Social Networks*, 22(2): 123–40.
Stone, D (2002) *Policy Paradox: The art of political decision making*, Norton, New York.
Stone, W (2001) *Measuring Social Capital*, Australian Institute of Family Studies, Melbourne.
Sullivan, H & Skelcher, C (2002) *Working Across Boundaries. Collaboration in Public Services*, Palgrave Macmillan, Houndmills.
Swift, F (1993) *Strategic management in the public service – the changing role of the deputy minister*, Canadian Centre for Management Development, Ottawa.
Szreter, S (2002) The state of social capital: Bringing back in power, politics and history, *Theory and Society*, 31(5): 573–621.
Taylor, M (2004) Community issues and social networks. In Chris Phillipson, Graham Allan & David HJ Morgan (eds) *Social Networks and Social Exclusion: Sociological and policy perspectives*, Ashgate Publishing, Aldershot: 205–18.
Teske, P & Schneider, M (1994) The bureaucratic entrepreneur: The case of city

managers, *Public Administration Review*, 54(4): 331–40.

Thompson, AM & Perry, JL (2006), Collaboration processes: Inside the black box, *Public Administration Review*, 66(S1): 20–32.

Thompson, GF (2003) *Between Hierarchies and Markets: The logic and limits of network forms of organization*, Oxford University Press, Oxford.

Thompson, GF, Frances, J, Levacic, R & Mitchell, J (eds) (1991) *Markets, Hierarchies and Networks: The coordination of social life*, Sage, London.

Thurmaier, K & Wood, C (2002) Interlocal agreements as overlapping social networks: Picket-fence regionalism in Metropolitan Kansas City, *Public Administration Review*, 62(5): 585–98.

UK Cabinet Office (1998) *Modernising government*, HMSO, London.

—— (2002) *Social Capital: A discussion paper*, Performance and Innovation Unit, London.

Valente, T (1998) *Network Models of the Diffusion of Innovations*, Hampton Press, Creskill NJ.

Valente, TW (1995) *Network Models of the Diffusion of Innovations*, Hampton Press, Cresskill NJ.

Van de Ven, AH & Rogers, EM (1988) Innovations and organisations – critical perspectives, *Communication Research*, 15: 632–51.

Van Der Gaag, M & Snijders, T (2005) The resource generator: Social capital quantification with concrete items, *Social Networks*, 27: 1–29.

Volker, B & Flap, H (1999) Getting ahead in the GDR: Social capital and status attainment under communism, *Acta Sociologica*, 42: 17–34.

Wagner, CS & Leydesdorff, L (2005) Network structure, self-organization, and the growth of international collaboration in science, *Research Policy*, 34: 1608–18.

Walker, JL (1969) Setting the agenda in the US Senate: A theory of problem selection, *British Journal of Political Science* 7: 433–45.

Walker, RM & Enticott, G (2004) Using multiple informants in public administration: Revisiting the managerial values and actions debate, *Journal of Public Administration Research and Theory*, 14(3): 417–34.

Walters, J (2001) *Understanding Innovation: What inspires it? What makes it successful?*, New Ways to Manage Series, PricewaterhouseCoopers Endowment for the Business of Government, http://www.endowment.pwcglobal.com.

Warr, D (2005) Social networks in a 'discredited' neighbourhood, *Journal of Sociology*, 41: 287–310.

—— (2006) Gender, class and the art and craft of social capital, *The Sociological Quarterly* 47(3): 497–520.

Wasserman, S & Faust, K (1994) *Social Network Analysis: Methods and applications*, Cambridge University Press, New York.

Wellman, B (1979) The community question: The intimate networks of east Yorkers, *American Journal of Sociology*, 84: 1201–31.

White, HC (1992) *Identity and Control: A structural theory of social action*, Princeton University Press, Princeton, NJ.

White, HC, Boorman, SA & Breiger, RL (1976). Social structure from multiple networks: 1. blockmodels of roles and positions, *American Journal of Sociology*, 81: 730–80.

Winter, I (ed.) (2000) *Social Capital and Public Policy in Australia*, Australian Institute of Family Studies, Melbourne.

Woolcock, M (1998) Social capital and economic development: Toward a theoretical

synthesis and policy framework, *Theory and Society*, 27(2): 151–208.
—— (2001) The place of social capital in understanding social and economic outcomes, *ISUMA: Canadian Journal of Policy Research*, 2(1): 11–17.
Woolcock, M & Narayan, D (2000) Social capital: Implications for development theory, research, and policy, *The World Bank Research Observer*, 15(2): 225–49.

Index

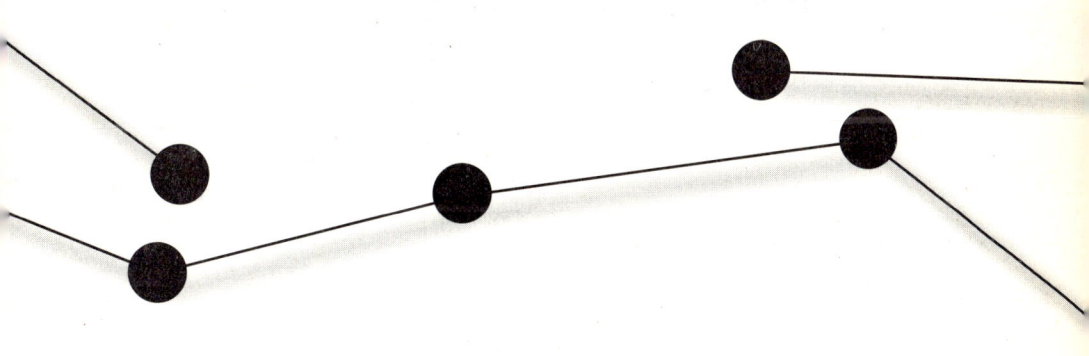

A
A Fairer Victoria policy 154
Aboriginal Medical Service 157
academic capitalism 169
academic collaboration
  co-authorship 170, 179–80, 190
    concerns with 180
  encouragement of 164–65, 182–85, 190–91
    funding incentives 164–65, 182, 189
    government policy 164–65, 182, 184–85, 190–91, 202
    institutional policy 182–85, 190–91
  grants for 164–65
  government policy 164–65, 182, 184–85, 190–91, 202
  failed collaborations 167
  Research Quality Framework 184–85
  sciences model of 182, 184–85
  shared values and 167
  types of 166
academic networks, *see also* academic collaboration; publication networks; research networks

benefits of 166–68, 190
career stage 187–88
  early career researchers 178, 179, 180, 181, 183, 184, 191
  senior researchers 181–84
dark side to 167–68
disciplinary differences 170–76, 185
disciplinary traditions 165–66, 169, 170, 179, 180, 181, 190, 202
  humanities 165, 181
  social sciences 181
government policy 165, 168, 169–70, 182, 184, 185, 202
heterophily 168
institutional context 169
intellectual curiosity and shared interests 165, 169, 181, 185
interviews 171, 176–77
knowledge generation 167–68, 170, 191
norms 167
performance frameworks 181, 185
power 167
publishing 166, 167, 179

• 219

shared values 167, 186
trust 167
academic prestige 169
  measurement of 169
action 25, 32, 35, 37, 38, 39–40, 42, 43, 45, 58, 196
  expressive 32, 39–40, 43, 196
  instrumental 32, 39, 40, 43, 196
actor constellation 53
Actor Network Theory 51
advice networks
  inside government 74, 75, 109, 114–15, 117–21, 123, 125–27
    bureaucrats 117, 120
    central actors in 119–21
    CEO's and mayor's ego 114–15, 117
    hierarchical position 118, 119, 120–21
    politicians 117, 119–21
advocacy coalitions, see policy networks
Age newspaper 92
agency 42, 47, 72, 139, 150, 155
Alexander, Damon 112, 138
Alford, Robert 80
Arneil, Barbara 19
Australia
  academic prestige in 169
  social capital policy 10–11, 64, 193
  general practitioners in 151
  health services in 98, 136, 157
  knowledge generation policy 164
  social and economic restructuring in 153
Australian Bureau of Statistics 68, 193
Australian Nursing Federation 88, 91
Australian Research Council 164–65

B
Baeza, Juan I 138
Baron, Stephen 63, 198
Blair Government 10
blockmodelling 86–87, 101, 103,
  see also health policy networks, influential actors 2001, blocks; health policy networks, influential actors 2004, blocks
bonding social capital 34, 41, 44, 46, 50, 65, see also bonding ties
bonding ties 34, 41, 44, 46, 50, 65, see also bonding social capital

Bourdieu, Pierre 25–30, 31, 32–33, 35, 37, 39, 40, 44, 54, 195–96
Bracks Government 135
bridging social capital 21–24, 33, 196, see also bridging ties
bridging ties, 32, 34, 41, 44, 46, 50, 54–55, 65, 74, 91, see also bridging social capital
brokerage 32, 55, 135, 196
brokers 32, 55, 75, 91, 133, 135, 137, 140, 141, 143, 152, 153, 155, 157–63, 201
  importance of to partnerships, 159–63, 201
Burt, Ronald S 16, 17, 20, 32, 35, 40, 41, 44, 45, 55, 193, 196, 198
Byrne, David 58

C
Campaspe 138, see also Campaspe Primary Care Partnership
  socio-economic characteristics 138
Campaspe Primary Care Partnership 138, 140–47, 148–53
  participant evaluations of 148–53
  strategic information networks 140–41, 142
    central actors in 140–41, 145, 146
    central organisations in 142
    structural change in 145, 146
  work networks 140–47
    central actors 140–41, 143, 145–46
    central organisations 142–43, 147
    structural change in 143–46, 147
Canadian Government 66
capital 18, 25–28, 31, 36, 39, 47, 70, 195
  accumulation of 26, 28, 33, 35, 50, 195–97
  as accumulated labour 26
  cultural capital 27, 36–38
  cultural reproduction 25–26
  economic capital 27, 28, 29
  human capital 27, 30, 34, 36–37, 38, 39, 43, 81
  intellectual capital 166
  physical capital 36
  power 18, 26
  social reproduction, 25–26

social capital, *see* social capital
Caroline Springs Partnership 156–58, 160–62
  key characteristics 157
  network maps and partnership evaluation 161–62
  role of broker in 160–61
  strategic information network 158, 160–61
centrality 74–75, 78, 89, 90–94, 99–105, 107, 118–27, 140–47, 151, 153, 163
  advice networks 118–27
  betweenness 74, 78, 80, 90–92, 104, 105, 107
  health influence networks 90–94, 99–105, 107
  in-degree 74, 75, 90–92, 99–104, 118–21, 140–47
  innovation inside government 118–127
  partnership networks 140–47, 151, 153, 163
  strategic information networks 118–27, 140–42, 143, 145, 146
  work networks 140–47
civic engagement 14
  government performance 14
civil society 10, 14, 19, 20, 22–24, 60–63, 65, 192, 195
  decline of 14, 20, 65, 192, 195, *see also* Putnam, decline thesis
  state–civil society relations 22–24, 60–63, 192
closure 20, 31, 32, 39, 40, 41, 55, 65–66, 108, 196
  and innovation 108
  and social support 32
  and status quo 32
Coleman, James S 16, 20, 25, 30–35, 29, 40, 44, 195, 196
Columbia University 170
  academic networks at 170
community 12, 19, 20, 60–61
Community Building Initiative 129
Community Development Partnerships 128–30, 153–63, 201
  background to 129–130, 153–55
  brokers 155, 158, 159–62, 163
    importance of 159–62, 163
    skills of successful 160–61

Caroline Springs Partnership
  broker in 160–61
  strategic information network 158, 160–61
  features of effective partnerships 158–63
  brokers 159–62, 163
  key characteristics of 157
  network maps and evaluation of 161–62
  research methods 155–56
  strategic information networks 155–56, 158, 160–61
  work networks 155–56
community strengthening 12, 154
Community Renewal Partnership 129
complexity 50, 55, 56–59, 60, 67
  public policy 59–60
  in science 57–58
  social capital 56–59
complexity theory 50, 56, 58–59, 197–98
  public policy 197–98
  social capital 56–59
communication networks, *see* advice networks; strategic information networks; work networks
community power studies 77
Considine, Mark 112
constructivism 12
Council of Australian Governments 129, 155, 157
cultural reproduction 25–26

D
Daly, Mary 70
Delfin Lend Lease 157, 161
dense networks, *see* closure
Department of Education 160
Department of Human Services 87–88, 92, 129, 137, 138, 145, 146, 147, 149, 152
Department of Planning and Community Development 129, 153, 154, 155, 157
Department of Victorian Communities 135
Division of General Practice 137, 146, 148, 151
Durlauf, Steven N 70

E

early career researchers 166, 178, 180, 181, 183, 184, 191
economics 18, 30
  and colonisation of the social sciences 62
elites 11, 32–33, 83, 95, 202
emergence
Europe
  social capital policy 61–62, 64
  social exclusion 61–62, 64, 194
ego networks 75, 76, 114–18, 174–76
  CEO's and mayor's advice 114–15, 117
  CEO's and mayor's strategic information 116–18
  political scientist's publication 174–75
  radiologist's publication 174, 176
embedded resources 36, 38–9, 40, 42, 43, 44–45, 47, 48, 76, 79, 81, 107, 110, 111, 127, 193, 202
expressive ties 17, 50, 76, 166, 187, 196

F

Fafchamps, Marcel 70
Faculty of Arts
  disciplines within 176
  publication networks 171–75, 182
  research networks 176–81
Faculty of Science
  publication networks 171–75, 182
Field, John 63, 65, 198
free-riding 18
Friedkin, Noah E 170

G

gatekeeper, *see* broker
general practitioners 137, 151
globalisation 153
governance 130, 131
  bureaucracies 130
  hierarchies 131, 132
  markets 130, 131, 132
  networks, *see* network governance
Granovetter, Mark 20, 22, 40, 44, 45, 54, 55, 196
Green, politics 119

H

habitus 37
Halpern, David 31

health partnerships, *see* Primary Care Partnerships
health policy networks 82–107
  influence network 85–86, 100–03
    blocks in 86–90, 101–03
    structural equivalence 86, 89, 90, 101
  influential actors 84–85, 90–94, 101–05
    centrality of 90–92, 104–05
    gender 85, 93
    identification of 82–85
    interviews with 90–92
    length of association with policy area 93
    medical qualifications 93
    network position 74, 92
    most difficult issues 96–100, 105–07
    most important issues 96–100, 105–07
    ongoing contact amongst 85–86
    preferential attachment 93
  issue networks
    proximity 78, 95
    influence and issue selection 99–100, 105–07
heterogeneous ties, *see* heterophilous ties
heterophilous ties 21, 32, 43–44, 46, 54, 82, 168, 196
  and instrumental action 32
  and resources 43–44, 54, 82
  and social class 44
heterophily, *see* heterophilous ties
HIV/AIDS 88
holism 56
homogenous ties, *see* homophilous ties
homophilous ties 21, 28, 32, 44, 46, 54, 82, 89, 186–87
  academic research networks 186–87
  expressive action 32
  resources 44, 46, 54, 82
homophily 42, 43, 54, 82, 86, 186
  academic research networks 186
  health policy influence network 86
  status quo 54
Howard Government 184

I

individualism 11, 182
influence

in health policy networks, *see* health policy networks
and network location 202–03
and policy agenda setting 77, 80–82, 199
information seeking
and organisational structure 109
innovation
  economic performance 108
  economic policy 108–109
  individual property, as an 110
  inside government 74, 108–14, 121–27, 199, *see also* innovation inside government
    bureaucrats 109, 112, 114–18, 119–21
    key innovators 121–27
    politicians 109, 112, 114–18, 119–121
    systems approach 110
  networks 65–66, 109, 110–11, 113–14, 126
  and innovation diffusion 110–11, 113
  policy making 110
  private sector 113
  public sector 113–14
  social capital 64–66, 108–11
innovation inside government 108–14, 121–27, 199
  advice networks, *see* advice networks
  case study municipalities
    interviews 121
    selection of 112, 119
    socioeconomic characteristics 119
    survey 112–13
  key innovators 121–27, 199
    advice centrality 122–27
    hierarchical position 122–27, 199
    network position 122–27, 199
    strategic information centrality 122–27
    strategic information networks, *see* strategic information networks
interconnectedness, *see* networks
interaction 56
International Network for Social Network Analysis 72
interviews 90, 101, 121, 156, 176–77

issue sets 100
Italy 14

J
Jessop, Bob 72
joined-up government 132, *see also* network governance

K
Kadushin, Charles 32
key innovators, *see* innovation inside government, key innovators
Kilbourne
  central actors 119–21
    and hierarchical position 120–21
  key innovators 121–22, 124–26
    and hierarchical position 122–26
    and network position 122–26
  socio-economic characteristics 119
Kingdon, John 79
knowledge generation, 75, 108, 164–65, 167, 168, 170, 182, 186, 190–91, 194, 201–02, 203–04

L
Labor, politics 119
Latin America
  social exclusion in 61
Laverton Community Renewal 157
Lewis, Jenny M 82, 112, 138, 154, 158
Lin, Nan 25, 32, 35–46, 48, 54, 55, 69, 193, 195, 196
linking social capital 22, 23–24, 55, 196, *see also* linking ties; social capital framework
  and civil society 23–24
  and power relations 23–24, 55
  and public policy 23–24
linking ties 46, 50, 65, *see also* linking social capital, social capital framework
local government 24, 112, 113–14, 160
  community development partnerships 129, 157, 161
  health services 136
  innovation in 113–14
  innovative capacity of 113
  Primary Care Partnerships, 137, 140–41, 142, 143, 146, 147, 151

Index • 223

reform of, Victoria 135
Lundvall, Bengt-Ake 110

M
Marx, Karl, *see* Marxist theory
Marxist theory 36–37
Melbourne 119, 138, 183
Melton Shire Council 157, 158
Melville
  central actors in 119–21
    and hierarchical position 120–21
  key innovators 121–22, 124–26
    and hierarchical position 122–26
    and network position 122–26
  socioeconomic characteristics of 119
Millside
  central actors in 119–21
    and hierarchical position 120–21
  key innovators 121–22, 124–26
    and hierarchical position 122–26
    and network position 122–26
  socioeconomic characteristics of 119
Mintrom, Michael 126
multiple regression 75, 122, 123–25
multivariate analysis 118–19, 122

N
name generators, *see* social network analysis, name generators
Nash, Vicki 66
National Health and Medical Research Council 164–65
neo–capital theory 36, 37, *see also* cultural capital; human capital
network analysis, *see* social network analysis
network governance 13, 51, 52, 53, 130–32, 134, 197
  partnerships 132–33
networks 29, 31, 32, 51–53, 60, 67, 71, 95, 197, *see also* advice networks; social network analysis; social networks; strategic information networks; work networks
  bridging networks, *see* bridging ties
  embedded resources, *see* embedded resources
  expressive 17, 50, 76, 166, 187, 196
  form of governance 29, 33–34, 51

individual attributes 186
inequality, *see* social capital, inequality
innovation, *see* innovation, networks
instrumental, *see* social capital framework, forms, instrumental
loose 32
managed 133
norms, *see* norms; social networks, norms
obligations 31
organisational structures 109, 186
policy agenda setting 82, 100, 110, 111
public policy, *see* social capital framework
resources, *see* embedded resources
role of government in building 154
self-generated 52
social capital, *see* social capital, networks
social class 21–22, 33–34
systems accounts 52
theory 43, 50, 51, 78
ties, *see also* social capital framework, forms of
  direct 43
  indirect 43
  multiplexity 69
  symbolic value of 43
unemployed 34, 54
values 81, 167, 186
nodes 52, 53, 54, 65, 93, 140, 199
non-government organisations, *see* not-for-profit organisations
norms, 10, 14, 15, 29, 30, 31, 40, 68, 79, 114, 119, 133, 167, 186, 193, 195
not-for-profit organisations 13, 85, 88, 89, 93, 101, 133, 136, 153, 157, 161
  and health policy networks 85, 88, 89, 93, 101
  and health services 136
  and partnerships 133, 153, 157, 161

O
Oberon
  CEO and mayor's advice network 114–15, 117
Organisation for Economic Cooperation and Development 194

P
Paldam, Martin 49
Parkside
  CEO and mayor's advice network 114–115, 117
  CEO and mayor's strategic information network 116–17, 118
  central actors 119–21
    and hierarchical position 120–21
  key innovators 121–26
    and hierarchical position 122–26
    and network position 122–26
  socioeconomic characteristics of 119
partnerships 66, 75, 128–35, 154, see also Caroline Springs Partnership; Community Development Partnerships; Primary Care Partnerships
  benefits of 134
  centrality 75
  community building partnerships, see Community Development Partnerships
  dark side to 134
  definitions of 128, 131, 132–33
  evaluation of 131, 134–35
  governance through 130, 132–33, see also network governance
  ideal characteristics of 163
  networks 134
  network centred approach to 163
  network maps as a diagnostic tool for 163
  place–based 66, 200–01
  Primary Care Partnerships, see Primary Care Partnerships
  public–private 128
  role of brokers in 75, 135
  role of government in 75, 129–30, 133–34
  service coordination partnerships, see Primary Care Partnerships
  social capital 130–31, 134, 135, 162–63, 201
  strategic information networks 75
  work networks 75
partnership facilitator 133, 158, see also brokers
Paxton, Pamela 15

Perri 6 66
personal resources, see capital, human capital
policy agenda setting 77–81, 82, 94–100, 108, 109, 199, see also health policy networks
  influence 77–79, 80–81, 199
    formal position 78, 82
    network position 74, 100, 107, 199, 202–03
    social capital approach to 77–79, 81, 94
    social networks and 77–79, 81, 82, 109, 110, 111–12, 199
  level of analysis 79
  proximity 78, 95
  social capital 95, 108
  structural equivalence 86, 89, 90, 101
policy communities, see policy networks
policy entrepreneur 79
policy field 78, 95, 109
policy issue networks 51, 95
policy making, see policy agenda setting
policy networks 51, 52–53, 54, 95, 197
  boundaries in 53
  functional interdependence 53
  nodes in 53
  ties in 53
policy process 51–53, 59–60, 74, 80, 100
  relational aspect of 60
  social capital 9
  social capital framework 45–47, 76, 81, 107, 112, 197–98, 200, 202, 204
political science, 52, 176
publication networks 171–76
  co-authorship 172–76
  disciplinary differences 171, 172, 174, 180
  Faculty of Arts 172–75
  Faculty of Science 172–76
  network analysis 172–76
  publication types 171–72
Pope, Jeanette 154–58
Portes, Alejandro 15, 17–18, 19, 20–21, 29, 34, 40, 56, 65
position generators, see social network analysis
power, 17, 18, 22, 26, 29, 30, 41, 55,

Index • 225

60, 62, 63, 74, 77, 78, 79, 80, 81, 82, 93, 94, 103, 110, 111–12, 134, 167, 195, 198
Primary Care Partnerships 129–30, 135, 136–53, 163
  background to 129–30, 135–37
  brokers 137, 140–41, 143
    importance of 152–53, 163
  core agencies 137
  Campaspe Primary Care Partnership, see Campaspe Primary Care Partnership
  participant evaluation of 148–53
  research methods
    interviews 138–39
    interview schedule 138–39
    network analysis 138–39
  role of government in 152–53
  social capital 129
  strategic information networks, see strategic information networks
  Westbay Primary Care Partnership, see Westbay Primary Care Partnership
  work networks, see work networks
Productivity Commission 10, 193
proximity 75, 78, 80, 95, 168, 185–88, 190
public policy, see also policy agenda setting; policy networks; policy process; social capital, policy analysis; social capital framework, public policy
  discourse of policy 60
  ideas 60
  knowledge generation 164–65, 191, 194, 201–02, 203–04
  mechanical models 59–60
  politics 59–60
  rational models 59
  relational aspect of 60
  social capital, building of, see social capital, role of government in building
public sector, reform of 131–32
publishing, see publication networks; research networks
Putnam, Robert D 9–10, 11, 13, 14–16, 18–25, 29, 30, 32, 39, 40, 65, 67, 68, 192, 193, 195, 196

Bowling Alone 9, 14, 23, 193, 195
  decline thesis 11, 14–15, 19, 20, 65, 192, 195
    appeal of to elites 11
    critique of 14–15, 19, 23, 195
  social capital index 67
    concerns with 67–68

R

rational choice 29, 35, 41, 44, 46, 49, 55, 79, 193, 196, 197
rationalism 12, 29
Regional Sports Assemblies 129
reputational survey 82–85
research clusters, see research networks
research culture 170, 179
research grants 164–65, 166, 167, 169, 170, 178–79, 190–81, 182–83, 189
research networks 164, 176–81, 185–86, 187–88, 190–91
  Faculty of Arts 176–81
  expressive 166, 187
  grants collaboration 179, 180–81
    career stage 179–81
    discipline 179–81
    drivers of 180–81
  gender 185–8, 190
  homophily 186–87
    gender 186–87
  interviews 176–77, 187, 188
  joint publishing 179–180
  knowledge generation 186, 190
  research groups 177–78
    activities of 177–78
    benefits of 178–79, 188–89
    concerns with 185
  proximity 168, 185–87, 188, 190
    gender 185–88, 190
  sole publishing 179–80
Research Quality Framework 184, 185
research policy 169–70, 190
resources
  and action, see action
  and authority 41–42, 44
  network ties 43, 111, see also embedded resources
  personal, see capital, human capital
  positional 43, 81, 93–94
  social 39, 81–82

and social structure 41, 42

S
Schuller, Tom 53, 198
seeing the network twice 72
Silver, Hilary 70
Snijders, Tom 70
snowball sampling 83–84, 103
sociability 14, 18, 19, 67
social capital
  academic networks 167, 202
  accumulation of 28, 33, 39–40
  ambiguity of 11, 31, 48, 192–93, 194
  benefits of 11, 66, 68, 194
  circularity of 35, 56, 57, 61, 65, 198
  civil society 19
  closure 32
  community building 12, 59
  complexity 50, 56, 197
  complexity theory 55, 57, 198
  convertibility of 27
  dark side of 17–18
  decline of, *see* Putnam, Robert D, decline thesis
  definitions of 10, 14–15, 16, 25, 27–28, 30–31, 38, 40, 48, 49, 193
  economic exchange 18
  economics-based view 18, 49
  embedded resources 30, 33, 36, 38, 40, 42, 44, 47, 50, 56, 193, 196, 202
  emotional investment 29
  forms, *see* social capital framework
  functions of 20
  gender 33–34
  heuristic value of 13, 64
  inequality 21–22, 29, 33–34, 62–63, 195
  influence 18, 29, 30
  innovation 109, 110–11
  issue sets 100
  knowledge generation 167–68, 182, 191, 194
  level of accumulation 15, 18, 35–35, 38, 39–40, 45–46, 47, 49, 50, 64–65, 79, 195–96, 197
  level of analysis 14–15, 18, 31, 34–35, 40, 45–46, 63–64, 68, 195
  methodological challenges 67–73, 199
  multi-level concept 46, 70

network position 50, 55, 193
network size 28
network structure 130
networks 10, 13, 14, 25, 27, 40, 42, 43, 48, 50, 56, 70, 193, 196, 197
norms 10, 30, 31, 193
obligations 27, 29, 31
partnerships 134–135, 162, 163, 200–201
policy analysis 9, 12–13, 22, 23–24, 47, 60, 94, 194–95, 197, 198, 202–03
policy influence 77, 78, 80, 81, 82, 84, 95, 127
popular appeal of 10, 51, 192, 193–94
public good 39
public good assumption 15, 17, 29, 30–31, 59, 195
purposeful action 25, 35, 40, 42, 44, 45, 47, 48, 50, 193, 196, 202
rational choice 29, 35, 41, 49, 55, 79, 193
reciprocity 14, 15, 25, 29, 193
relational aspect of 55, 56, 68, 199
role of government in building 10–11, 19, 22–23, 53, 55, 60–62, 63, 64, 66, 73, 74, 129, 154, 190–91, 193–94, 195, 198–203
sanctions 31
sociability 18
social class 21–22, 26, 33–34, 39
social networks 14, 15, 25, 36, 40, 42, 43, 48, 56, 70, 73, 193
social network analysis 69, 197, *see also* social network analysis
social stratification 36, 33
social structure 32, 45, 47
state–civic relations, *see* civil society, state–civil relations
structural position 16, 17
time dimension of 47, 50
titles 27
trust 14, 16–17, 29, 30, 31, 193, 195, *see also* trust
values 31, 41, 64
Social Capital: A Theory of Social Structure and Action 35
social capital framework 45–47, 49–50, 60, 72, 111, 129, 194–95, 196–97

Index • 227

complexity theory 56–59, 197–98
forms of
  bonding ties 34, 41, 44, 46, 50, 65
  bridging ties 32, 34, 41, 44, 46, 50, 65
  expressive ties 17, 50, 76, 166, 187, 196
  instrumental ties 46, 50, 71, 196
  interactions between 50, 196–97
  linking ties 46, 50, 65
  strong ties 32, 39, 44, 46, 54
  weak ties 20, 22, 34, 44, 45, 46, 54, 196
level of accumulation 15, 18, 35, 38, 40, 46, 47, 49, 50, 64–65, 79, 195–96, 197
level of analysis 14–15, 18, 19, 37–38, 40, 49, 50, 64, 67–68, 79, 94, 107, 195, 196
  interactions between 49, 50, 196–97
policy agenda setting 79, 80, 82
public policy 59–67, 73, 107, 196, 199–200, 203
  methodological challenges 199
social networks, *see* social networks
social class 25, 36–37, 39
  human capital 36–37
  social capital 21–22, 26, 33–34, 39
social connectedness, *see* networks
social exclusion 61–62, 194
  appeal of concept 62
  policy
    Europe 61–62, 194
    Latin America 61
    United Kingdom 194
  states 61–62
Social Exclusion Unit 66
social networks 14, 15, 17, 20, 25, 36, 38, 40, 42, 48, 52, 56, 58, 65–66, 70–73, 109, 111–13, 118, 193–97
  and embedded resources 36, 38, 39, 40, 42, 48, 79, 110, 111, 127, 197, 202
  gender 19–20, 186
  government innovation 109
  individual mobility 15
  norms 14, 15, 29, 31, 114, 167, 186, 193
  reciprocity 14, 15, 25, 193

social capital 14, 15, 25, 36, 40, 42, 43, 48, 56, 70, 73, 193
social resources 16, 39, 81–82
theory 42–43, 50, 51
trust 14, 15, 16–17, 29, 53, 54, 167, 193, 195
social network analysis 51, 53–54, 68–72, 83, 85, 139, 197, 199, 203
agency 72
blockmodelling 86–87, 101, 103
boundaries 53, 54, 84
descriptive statistics 72
level of analysis 53–54, 197
name generators 69, 70, 83, 114
nodes 52–54, *see also* nodes
policy analysis 197, 199, 203, 204
position generators 69–70
proximity 75, 78, 80, 95, 168, 185–88, 190
qualitative data 70
relational data 47, 68, 71, 85, 86
resource generators 70
social capital measurement 69, 199
strategic–relational approach 72
ties 52–54, *see also* social capital framework, forms
social sciences 18, 64, 170, 171, 180, 181, 190
  colonisation of 18
social status, *see* social class
society, *see also* civil society
  definition 37
  economic view
  network 62
socioeconomic status 119
sociology 18, 30, 176
statistical analysis 71
strategic information networks 114, 116–17, 140–41, 142, 145, 146, 158
  Caroline Springs Partnership 158, 160–61
  inside government 114, 116–117, 118, 126
    bureaucrats 117, 120
    central actors in 118–21
    CEOs and mayors ego 114, 116–18
    hierarchy 118–21
    politicians 117, 120–21
  Primary Care Partnerships 140–147,

see also Campaspe Primary Care Partnership; Westbay Primary Care Partnership
strong ties 32, 39, 44, 46, 54
structural equivalence 74, 80, 86, 89–90, 101, 102
structural holes 20, 32, 44, 55
structure–agency relationship 37–38, 45, 47, 50, 72, 155
surveys 82–85, 112–13
  and relational data 68–69
symbolic violence 37
Szreter, Simon 19, 21–22, 23, 24, 40, 62, 201

T
Thatcher, Margaret 192
third who benefits, see brokers
ties, see social capital framework, forms
Transport Connections 129
  partnership 157
trust 10, 14–17, 19, 29, 30, 31, 53, 54, 67–68, 79, 81, 133, 148, 152, 161, 167, 179, 193, 195
  measurement of 67–68
  mistrust 17
  versus mutual affection 16

U
United Kingdom
  public sector reform 131–32
  social capital policy 10, 65, 66, 193–94
United States
  community in 61–62
  decline of civil society, see civil society, decline of
  social capital policy 170
University of Chicago 170
  academic networks at 170
University of Melbourne 91, 104, 171

V
values, social 20, 31, 37, 41, 64, 81, 166, 167, 186
van der Gaag, Martin 70
Vergari, Sandra 126
VicHealth 91, 92, 101, 104–05
Victoria
  health policy networks, see health policy networks
  local government, see innovation inside government
  partnerships, see community development partnerships; partnerships; primary care partnerships
Victorian government 154
Victorian Local Governance Association 112

W
Wallerstrum 116–18
  CEO and mayors strategic information network 116–18
Warr, Deborah 33
weak ties 20, 22, 34, 44, 45, 46, 54, 196
Westbay, see also Westbay Primary Care Partnership
  socio-economic characteristics 138
Westbay Primary Care Partnership 138, 140–43, 145–47, 148–53
  participant evaluations of 148–53
  strategic information network 140–41, 142
    central actors 140–41, 145, 146–47
    central organisations 142, 147
    structural change 145, 146, 147
  work network 140–43, 145, 146, 147
    central actors 140–41, 145, 146–47
    central organisations 142–43, 147
    structural change 145, 146, 147
whole of government approach 132
Winter, Ian 61
Woolcock, Michael 18, 22, 55, 61, 62, 64
work networks 140–47
  Campaspe Primary Care Partnership
    central actors in 140–41, 143–46
    central organisations in 142–43, 147
    structural change 143–45, 146
  Westbay Primary Care Partnership
    central actors in 140–41, 145, 146
    central organisations in 143–43, 147
    structural change 145, 146
World Bank 10, 18, 62, 194
World Values Survey 68